The
EVERYTHING
CAREER TESTS
BOOK

Dear Reader,

When I was fourteen, I wanted to be an orthodontist. For the next six years, I studied biology, chemistry, calculus, physics, and anatomy. But I also loved history, literature, art, and theater. I was a reader and a good writer, but I didn't know what to do with a love of literature. Orthodontics was tangible—and lucrative. In my junior year of college, I faced the truth: Teeth weren't my passion. I just didn't know how to make a living out of what I loved.

As a result, I floundered as a not-very-good secretary, newspaper type-setter, and waitress before I discovered the museum profession, which combined all of the interests, skills, and values so dear to my heart. Now as a freelance writer of books and museum exhibitions, I also get to write about every subject under the sun. I have found my niche.

Had I the sagacity to consult a career counselor at the beginning of my search, I would have saved myself a lot of time and angst. Now you, dear readers, can find all of the advice I lacked in the easy-to-use tool that you hold in your hands.

All you have to do is begin.

A. Bronwyn Llewellyn

The EVERYTHING® Series

Editorial

Publisher	Gary M. Krebs
Director of Product Development	Paula Munier
Managing Editor	Laura M. Daly
Associate Copy Chief	Sheila Zwiebel
Acquisitions Editor	Lisa Laing
Development Editor	Jessica LaPointe
Associate Production Editor	Casey Ebert

Production

Director of Manufacturing	Susan Beale
Associate Director of Production	Michelle Roy Kelly
Prepress	Erick DaCosta
	Matt LeBlanc
Design and Layout	Heather Barrett
	Brewster Brownville
	Colleen Cunningham
	Jennifer Oliveira
Series Cover Artist	Barry Littmann

Visit the entire Everything® Series at *www.everything.com*

THE
EVERYTHING®
CAREER
TESTS
BOOK

**10 tests to determine
the right occupation for you**

A. Bronwyn Llewellyn with Robin Holt, M.A.

Adams Media
Avon, Massachusetts

*To all of my colleagues, past, present, and future. They have all helped
make my career satisfying and fulfilling.*

The Accidental Entrepreneur: Practical Wisdom for People Who Never Expected to Work for Themselves, by Susan Urquart-Brown, found at *www.careersteps123.com/BOOK /bookDescription.html;* Elevations™, The Career Discovery Tool, published by Scully Career Associates, Inc. at *www.ElevateYourCareer.com;* Terry Karp, Value Search Coauthor, Principal and Career Consultant at the Bay Area Career Center in San Francisco, CA; Mark Guterman, Value Search Coauthor, Career Consultant at the Bay Area Career Center in San Francisco, CA

An Everything® Series Book.
Everything® and everything.com® are registered trademarks of F+W Publications, Inc.

Published by Adams Media, an F+W Publications Company
57 Littlefield Street, Avon, MA 02322 U.S.A.
www.adamsmedia.com

ISBN 10: 1-59337-565-4
ISBN 13: 978-1-59337-565-2

Printed in the United States of America.

J   I   H   G   F   E   D   C   B   A

Library of Congress Cataloging-in-Publication Data
available from the publisher

This publication is designed to provide accurate and authoritative information with regard to the subject matter covered. It is sold with the understanding that the publisher is not engaged in rendering legal, accounting, or other professional advice. If legal advice or other expert assistance is required, the services of a competent professional person should be sought.

—From a *Declaration of Principles* jointly adopted by a Committee of the
American Bar Association and a Committee of Publishers and Associations

Many of the designations used by manufacturers and sellers to distinguish their products are claimed as trademarks. Where those designations appear in this book and Adams Media was aware of a trademark claim, the designations have been printed with initial capital letters.

*This book is available at quantity discounts for bulk purchases.
For information, please call 1-800-289-0963.*

Contents

Acknowledgments

The authors gratefully acknowledge the contributions and support of Lisa Laing, Jessica LaPointe, Paula Munier, and everyone at Adams Media; Joan Ishiwata; as well as the generosity of Mark Guterman, Terry Karp, Jennifer Robinson, Dena Sneider, Helen M. Scully, and Susan Urquhart-Brown.

Top Ten Things to Remember about Career Tests

1. Most people hate taking tests.

2. Tests provide ideas, not blueprints.

3. Tests can be wrong.

4. No single test gives you all the answers.

5. You are a unique individual, not a category.

6. Tests can help you focus your choices.

7. Change is the one constant in life.

8. You should retake tests throughout your career.

9. Taking tests is the easy part.

10. Trust your instincts.

Introduction

▶ YOU WANT A satisfying career. That's probably why you're reading this book. It's safe to say that you want to work at something that provides an adequate income on which to live. But money isn't the only concern when it comes to a career. There's more to life than what you do for a living (if you need convincing, check out Chapters 4 and 8). Your health, your family and friends, and what you do in your downtime are vitally important to your overall well-being and your existence as a well-rounded person. With that said, this book is about careers and helping you find, adjust, and enhance yours so that it fits into that well-rounded existence. Ideally, your career should mesh with your desires—for success, fulfillment, accomplishment, whatever motivates you—which are unique and important to you.

Do you think your great-grandparents would recognize many of today's career options: Multimedia developer? Software engineer? Steganographer? Pet therapist? Genetic counselor? Perhaps the myriad opportunities overwhelm you, and you haven't settled on one yet. Maybe you feel dissatisfied or underappreciated in the career you currently have—even if it's one you trained long and hard to get. It's possible that you love your career but need a fresh challenge. You may just be wondering if your job situation is the best possible fit for you. How can you tell?

The answer lies in figuring out what you really want by assessing yourself and your situation right now. That status check will help you find out if you're in the best possible situation for you. It will even help you figure out what else is out there that might suit you. There are probably many options you haven't even thought of yet.

You don't have to wait until you're unhappy in your career to do a self-assessment. You wouldn't go to the doctor only when you have a life-threatening illness, would you? Nor should you evaluate your work situation only after things grow intolerable. In fact, that's probably the worst time to do it because desperation and unhappiness will cloud your judgment. Every five to ten years you should take the time to step back and re-evaluate where you are, where you're going, and how you're doing in terms of goals, benchmarks, satisfaction, fulfillment, and salary. Just as you check your pulse during aerobic activity to make sure it stays in the optimum range, so you should also check the pulse of your career to keep it humming along.

If there's one certainty in life, it's that people change. During the course of your working life you can be sure that your interests, desires, and life circumstances will change. These shifts will affect your career—the career you have as well as the career you want. You may need to make drastic career adjustments or you may not. Often all that you need is a little fine-tuning or a modest tweak or two. Perhaps you're ready to develop yourself as a manager, something you never would have considered a few years ago. Maybe it's time to launch your own entrepreneurial enterprise and be your own boss. On the other hand, you may feel that you are in the perfect career for you but want to ramp it up a notch. That should be very good news! What a relief to not be concerned with how green that grass is on the other side of the fence.

A few self-administered tests later, you could have clearer answers. After filling in the chart at the end of this book, you will have a better idea of where you are right now, where you're headed, and where to put the emphasis in your career trajectory. This book won't tell you what job to do or what career path you should take. The days of "trait and factor" career guidance are long gone. Instead, you will find things to adjust, things to overhaul, and new opportunities in which you can grow. You'll discover some surprising things about yourself that you didn't know before. You'll also have fun.

It was Ralph Waldo Emerson who wrote, "What lies behind us and what lies before us are tiny matters compared to what lies within us." Check out the next page and begin your exploration of the career that lies within you.

Chapter 1

Know Yourself, Know Your Career

When you were young, did you know what you wanted to be when you grew up? Are you in that career now? Maybe not, if you're reading this. Some people never know what career they want, but most people change during their working years. Some outgrow their careers, others shift priorities, and still others find new interests. Twenty-six centuries ago, a wise Athenian named Solon lived by the motto "Know thyself." Today, that bit of advice is the single best thing you can do to find or improve your career.

Self-Assessment Is Key

You may be in college and just starting to think about a career. Perhaps you've already had a succession of jobs that didn't seem to fit or satisfy you. It's possible that you're in a career you love but you need to change the way you work, such as going from full-time to part-time. Maybe you need to re-energize your career, whether by refining your goals or increasing your responsibilities. You may want to move to a different organization or city or stay right where you are but change departments. It's conceivable that you need a complete career overhaul.

The key to addressing each of these situations is assessing who you are, what you can already do or want to learn how to do, and what you really want. Once you have figured all of that out, you have a greater likelihood of making career decisions that will help you stay challenged, keep motivated, and be fulfilled as you progress through your working life. Yes, it's going to take some effort, but as that wise observer Anonymous noted, "If we are not willing to spend the energy toward creating what we want, we get to spend the same amount of energy coping with what we get."

Finding Your Passion

In generations past, people didn't have as many career options, or at least they didn't think they did. If a man worked for the electric company, chances were that his sons would, too. Daughters of homemaker mothers were supposed to follow suit. It didn't really matter if a child loved to draw, dissect lizards, or build models. If the family owned a grocery store, the children were expected to one day join the business or enter some other "suitable" profession, such as teaching. People loyally stayed with an employer for decades, nose to the grindstone, until they could collect the gold watch and pension and fade away into the sunset of retirement. Not any more.

Workers Have Changed

It used to be that the exception was the person who knew there was something that she was meant to do and went after it. Today that can describe anyone, but fewer people than you might think really follow their passion. A 2005 Harris Interactive, Inc. survey found that only 20 percent of U.S. workers feel passionate about their jobs. Would that we all could share the singleness of purpose of filmmaker Roger Corman. He was enamored of movies, but because his father wanted him to be an engineer, he graduated with an engineering degree. Just days into his new job, he knew he had to make movies, so he quit and moved to Hollywood. Corman became one of the most successful filmmakers in history because he followed his passion.

That same 2005 survey found that 21 percent of workers are eager to change careers and 33 percent feel as though their careers are at a dead end. Many of those people longing for change probably ended up where they are because they took an opportunity that arose with no thought as to whether or not they could do it—or even liked it. Sometimes that's just what you have to do to keep a roof over your head and food on the table. Many of those other dissatisfied people no doubt took jobs they enjoyed at the time—perhaps they even felt passionate about them—only to find out later that those jobs no longer suited their changed circumstances, perspectives, or interests.

Careers Have Changed

Choice in all aspects of life has increased exponentially, from what kind of car to drive to what detergent to use to which artisan bread to have with your soup. If you don't choose, the choice will be made for you, whether by default, circumstances beyond your control, or someone else. The same holds true for careers. The job market offers a vast array of exciting and seemingly limitless options. But behind all that wonderful variety lie important decisions to be made. Are you meant to be a greeting card writer or podiatrist? Architect or computer engineer? Translator or flight attendant? Lepidopterist or veterinarian? Kindergarten teacher or social worker? Policeman or park ranger? Corporate president or entrepreneur? When you really think about it, a vast number of choices can be paralyzing, not liberating. You could flip a coin, but that method isn't likely to result in a career that suits you or one that you feel passionate about.

If you are searching for more than a job, or if you want a satisfying career that uses your talents and abilities and engages your heart as well as your mind, then it's going to require some introspection—and decision-making—

on your part. The best way for you to find one of the careers that is perfect for you is to take a good honest look at yourself.

Self-Assessment Is Your Personal Checkup

If you are conscious about your health, you probably have a physical once per year. During this routine checkup, the doctor measures your height, weight, and blood pressure. Perhaps the exam includes an inspection of your eyes, hearing, skin, and reflexes. The doctor may press on your abdomen, tap on your back, or take X-rays to look at your lungs. Finally, lab tests check levels of cholesterol, enzymes, sugar, or platelets. The checkup provides a baseline of where your health is now. You may be healthy, but the tests will show you what you need to watch out for and what to change or tweak in order to stay healthy or get fit.

This book is designed to help you conduct a checkup of your values, skills and abilities, personality, creativity, and lifestyle and work preferences. Step by step, you will answer questions or make choices in a series of self-assessment instruments. Then you'll record your answers in the chart found at the end of the book. The result will be a snapshot of you right now that can then be used to determine your next steps toward finding a new career or customizing the career you have, with the ultimate purpose of achieving greater career-related satisfaction.

You are unique on this planet, with your own interests, values, and predilections. The teacher and author Joseph Campbell recognized the value that individuality gives to the world. He knew our contributions had to spring from "our own experiences and fulfillment of our own potentialities, not someone else's." There is no "one-size-fits-all" when choosing a career. It's a personal, highly subjective decision that is based on a set of criteria. Finding out what those criteria are is the purpose of *The Everything® Career Tests Book.*

Your Readiness for Change

You may be looking for a whole new career, but there are other reasons to do a self-assessment. There are lots of ways that you can improve your career without changing it completely. Put a check next to any of the following that describe you.

▶ **You're burned out.** That fire you exhibited for your job years ago is now little more than an ember. You gave it your all for as long as you could, and now, although you still like your career field, your current situation feels more like a treadmill than a career.

▶ **Your job is hazardous to your health.** Some jobs are dangerous, and if you're in one that is, you probably knew that when you signed on. Some jobs can affect your health in other ways, such as by being too stressful or emotionally draining, and those are things you may not have known when you took it.

▶ **You want to specialize.** You're in a career you love, but you want to focus on one specific aspect of it.

▶ **You're bored.** By midafternoon, you're watching the clock. You miss the intellectual challenge that you used to find in your work and are now just going through the motions.

▶ **You want more autonomy.** You are quite happy working by yourself at your own pace, without someone else telling you what to do or checking to make sure you're doing it.

▶ **Your personal situation has changed.** Big adjustments such as getting married, having kids, or caring for an ailing parent can change your priorities and affect how you view your career.

▶ **You want to advance.** Perhaps you have been promoted as far as you can go in your present job, but you know you have much more to offer and crave more responsibility.

▶ **You can see the writing on the wall.** Maybe you're in a field without much future, your company's about to be bought out, or the economy is taking a toll on your industry and it's time for you to move on.

▶ **You want more money.** Perhaps your responsibilities have increased but your salary has stayed the same. A 2005–2006 Salary.com, Inc. survey measuring employee satisfaction found that less than 50 percent of respondents believed they were adequately paid. The same survey revealed that inadequate compensation ranks as the biggest reason people leave their jobs. However, just because someone believes he is underpaid doesn't mean he is, relative to his peers. There are many other things besides money that can help one feel adequately compensated, from more vacation time to appropriate recognition.

▶ **You want more creativity.** You long for an opportunity that lets you think outside the box or dream up new things rather than adhere to a strict "we've always done it this way" mentality.

You May Not Be Ready for Change

If you checked one or two items, you are doing pretty well where you are. No job situation is perfect. It's the lucky person who has found a career that satisfies every one of her goals, needs, and desires. But if you feel strongly about one or two of these things, you can take the self-assessment tests in this book and map out some ways to approach your career differently.

You May Be Ready for Change

If you checked three to six items, you're probably ready for a change. You're in luck. The rest of the assessment tools in this book will help you figure out what that change might be and point you in the direction of implementing it. Remember, "change" doesn't necessarily mean changing careers or employers, although that may very well be what you want or need. There are many tweaks and improvements that can increase your career satisfaction in your present situation.

You Are Ready for Change

If you checked seven or more items, you are already in a career transition whether you realize it or not. Plodding on without making any changes at all won't do you—or your employer—any favors. If you know you need to do something but you're at a loss as to where to start, the self-assessment tools that follow will give you plenty of ideas as you set goals and take the necessary steps to reach them.

Why Take Self-Assessment Tests?

Tests are tools, and tools are labor-saving devices, a means to an end. Self-assessment tests, or career instruments, are just some of the means to help you find the career in which you can flourish and succeed. The average person changes careers several times in his or her lifetime. Sometimes you can call the shots and dictate the changes on your own schedule, but other times those changes get made for you by forces outside your control, such as the economy, employers, or unforeseen circumstances. Clarifying your goals, desires, and abilities will make such changes easier to navigate.

Susan was blindsided when her company laid her off in 2002. In retrospect, her employer did her a big favor, releasing her from a technical writing job that bored her and freeing her to spend more time writing fiction. Today, she has a half-dozen published books to her credit, but she realizes that if she'd taken the time to assess her passion and talents years before, she could have begun enjoying that career much earlier.

Make Informed Decisions

Self-assessment can help you clarify what you value in a job and what's important to you in your life and work. It can also indicate abilities and interests you know you have, as well as some that might surprise you. Nearly 400 years ago, British philosopher Francis Bacon wrote, " . . . knowledge itself is power. The more one knows, the more one will be able to control events."

Juan had a job in sales for a well-known beverage company. He worked from home and submitted his reports online, so he rarely went to the office or interacted with anyone from the company. He often found it hard to get going in the morning. It wasn't until he took some career assessment tests that he realized he was an extrovert and needed to be energized by other people before he could make sales calls. Once Juan no longer worked from home, he became the top salesman at his new job.

Focus Your Efforts and Resources

You may be thinking that you don't have the time to take ten tests or that they're too much work. In fact, the opposite is true. Taking these tests thoughtfully and honestly will save you time in the long run. It will save you needless effort chasing one possible career path after another or trying out options that really aren't a good fit for you because you have no idea what a good fit for you is. Of course, after you complete your self-assessment you may still want to pursue a career that isn't suggested by your test results, but at least you'll make that decision with more self-awareness and an idea of what you need to do in order to make it work.

Sarah seemed to jump to a new job every year: waiting tables, retail sales, preschool teaching, receptionist. When she finally stopped to assess her skills and abilities, Sarah discovered that she really didn't like working with the public. This revelation led her to find a more appropriate and satisfying job as a bookkeeper.

Focus Your Choices

You know how you feel when confronted with a menu of 200 items in a Chinese restaurant. Your mouth waters as you savor the possibilities, but you have to choose just one. Meanwhile, the waiter is tapping his pencil on his pad. Suddenly, it dawns on you that all of those choices aren't really choices for you. You're allergic to oranges, you hate broccoli, and you gave up noodles for Lent. Let's see, that narrows it down to . . . 152. And the waiter is still tapping his pencil.

Searching for a satisfying career can be a bit like that, though with many more far-reaching consequences. The wrong dinner can make you unhappy—or sick to your stomach—for the evening, but it's not the end of the world. The wrong career can leave you feeling unhappy, dissatisfied, and unfulfilled, feelings that have an insidious way of creeping into the rest of your life. You may never even know why you feel that way.

Carl had worked hard in school and landed a job with a top accounting firm. He kept telling himself how lucky he was, but at the same time, he felt blue and often had a hard time going to work on Monday mornings. After working with a career counselor, he discovered that accounting wasn't a good fit for him. Once he moved to a job in the human resources department, Carl knew he was on the right path.

Increase Your Choices

Once you narrow your scope to the career or careers that are best for you, you may find entire fields you never before considered. You may discover that you have an affinity for negotiating, mechanical drawing, or statistics that until now lay untapped and ignored because of a preconceived notion that you were "supposed" to be doing something completely different with your life.

Some people believe there is only one soul mate out there for them, one perfect, predestined partner, if only they could find him or her. In reality, the opposite is probably true, and once you believe that, your chances of finding one of those many potentially suitable partners increases dramatically. You just need to know who you are and what you're looking for. The same holds true for careers. Based on your interests, abilities, values, and preferences, there are several suitable niches for you, not just one "perfect" career. Remember, too, that you can focus, customize, and personalize any given career. Keep an open mind as you conduct your self-assessment and you will see opportunities as they arise.

Brenda worked as an administrative assistant in a large university hospital that offered its employees a course in self-assessment. She learned that she had a natural inclination toward and interest in the sciences. She decided to go back to school at night and take the necessary courses to become a scientific researcher. Eventually, Brenda was offered a research job in a laboratory that she felt was just the right fit for her.

Provide a Starting Point

People change. Remember that most working Americans will change careers several times. Taking these tests will give you a baseline of your skills, abilities, and values today. No one is saying that these won't change; undoubtedly they will. People burn out, decide they want or need more money, or modify their goals. That's why you should re-evaluate yourself periodically. It would be silly, if not hazardous to your health, to have a physical exam at age twenty and never set foot in a doctor's office again. Nor would you neglect regular tuneups for your car. Finding satisfaction in your life's work is certainly no less important, and figuring out where you are now can help you figure out where you're headed and how to get there.

Marilyn knew she wanted to pursue a career in education, but she'd seen her mother burn out as a classroom teacher. A self-assessment class at her college helped identify Marilyn's leadership and administrative skills, as well as her teaching ability. This information helped her realize that if she tired of classroom teaching, she could go back to school and earn an administrative credential.

What You Can Learn from These Tests

The ultimate purpose of all of these tests is to help you better understand yourself and your relationship with the working world. Armed with this self-knowledge, you will be able to make well-informed decisions that will affect your future happiness, satisfaction, and success in your chosen career. You have undoubtedly thought about some of these topics a lot, such as your values and your interests. The act of writing them down in your chart will help you see how they relate to your other characteristics—and how they correspond to possible careers.

Career Test Topics

You may never have given any thought to some of the other topics, such as the balance you want between your work and personal life or if you have what it takes to open your own business. By taking those tests, you will learn something new about yourself. You will gather more information that, when combined with all of your other test results, will help you clarify your career direction and decisions. The key is to take several tests. No single one will give you the help you are looking for, but all of your results together will round out a portrait of you and your preferences and enable you to more closely match your career options to that self-portrait.

Criteria for Job Satisfaction

This checklist gives you a preliminary glimpse at how you feel right now about making changes to your career. It indicates some of the types of possible changes.

Values

What do you value most in your career: Financial security? Helping others? Status? Loyalty? Depending on how you feel now, a career that resonates with your values can affect your feelings of satisfaction.

Skills

Perhaps you have a talent for managing people, computer programming, or improvising solutions on the fly. You stand a better chance of finding fulfillment in a career that uses your skills. Don't forget those skills that are related to your hobbies, too. You may dismiss them as unimportant, but many fulfilling careers started out as pastimes.

Interests

If you know you like to build things, be outdoors, or work with kids, you will probably enjoy a career that takes full advantage of your particular interests.

Personality

Knowing whether you are, for example, adventurous, spontaneous, structured, or serious can help you find work situations that suit your personality.

Work Environment

Perhaps you like a noisy, busy office environment with lots of people interacting, or you like to work outdoors. A desirable commute ranks very high among factors that keep employees happy in their jobs. Matching your preferences with your work environment can make or break your career satisfaction.

Location

This is about where in the country—or the world—you want to work, taking into account such considerations as climate, access to nature, affordability, and the livability of the location you choose. You don't always have a choice of where you'll work, but if you do, it's good to know your own preferences.

Work-Life Balance

Do you relish putting in seventy-hour weeks at the office, or would you prefer to have afternoons free to play with the kids after school? Perhaps you feel strongly about making time for volunteer work. Striking the right balance between your personal life and your professional life can have a huge impact on your career satisfaction.

Entrepreneurial Readiness

Are you a self-confident risk-taker who doesn't mind investing many hours and your own money in your business, or do you prefer receiving a regular paycheck for working a set number of hours? Not everyone is suited for the world of self-employment, but if you've never thought about it as an option before, you may surprise yourself.

Managerial Suitability

Are you a born leader? You may never have supervised other people before but still have the qualities of an excellent manager. This test will help you figure out your leadership potential.

Emotional Intelligence

You may be smart and you may have loads of technical skills, but if you don't have emotional intelligence, career success may elude you. Find out what it is and how to improve yours.

What These Tests Don't Do

These tests will not match you to any one particular career or job. These tests won't provide information about anyone else. Nor will they tell you if you can afford to make any of the suggested changes or how a particular career path will affect your relations with family or significant others. Those are determinations you will have to make on your own. No test or series of tests can give you all of the answers to your career questions. If, after taking the tests in this book, you are still unclear or need more direction, try looking at some in-depth publications relating to the careers that interest you, visit a few career Web sites, or consult a career counseling professional who can guide your further efforts at self-assessment, job hunting, and beyond. The resources listed in the appendices will help you.

How to Take the Tests

For some of you, these may be the first tests you have taken in years, if not decades. Relax. This isn't punishment, and the tests will be fun. After all, they concern the most fascinating topic in the world—you! Remember to photocopy the pages before you write on them so you can take the tests again in the future.

- Be rested.
- Find a quiet place with minimal distractions.
- Be comfortable.
- Read all instructions carefully.
- Answer honestly.
- Don't agonize over your responses. There are no right or wrong answers.
- Don't try to second-guess your responses.
- Take your time.

Sum Up Your Results

On pages 178–179, there is a chart where you can record your results from all of the tests in this book. When completely filled out, the chart will give you an easy-to-read, convenient, and current snapshot of you that will help you determine your next steps and focus your path to career fulfillment. The terminology used throughout this book is the same as that used by career counseling professionals, so you will be able to compare your results with other resources and literature in the field. Again, you may want to write on a photocopy of the chart so you can use it again in the future.

Career Change Options

If you are beginning to panic, thinking that your only choice is to completely change careers, relax. Change can take many forms, not all of them extreme. According to the poet T. S. Eliot, "People are only influenced in the direction in which they want to go, and influence consists largely in making them conscious of their wishes to proceed in that direction." The point here is to get you to begin to think hard about exactly what it is that you want to do. You may believe you have no idea, but on some level you probably do know. Try to let go of preconceived notions and timeworn expectations about yourself. Sometimes you have to take a risk in order to grab an opportunity. Listen to your heart, back it up with honest self-assessment and good research, and be confident that you will make the right decisions. Remember, there are no quick fixes to career change. You've already invested considerable time, energy, and money getting to where you are today. Your future career satisfaction is worth some focused attention now.

Following are some of the potential changes you could make to your career. Each item on this list represents many, many possibilities, from taking classes to taking on more job responsibilities, from moving to a new position within the same company to moving across the country to start a job in a completely new discipline. You will discover what your possibilities are as you complete your self-assessment. This is your starting point.

Put a checkmark in front of the choice that makes the most sense to you and your situation right now.

Right now, I think I want to . . .

- ❑ **Revitalize my current job.**
- ❑ **Make a change in the way I work.**
- ❑ **Make an internal move where I am now.**
- ❑ **Make a move to a new organization, location, or industry.**
- ❑ **Make a complete career change.**

After you complete the other tests in this book, you will revisit these same options to see if your thoughts about your career have changed. Now begin the process of discovering more about your values.

Chapter 2
Values and Your Career

Ice cream moguls Ben Cohen and Jerry Greenfield maintained, "We cannot suspend our values during the workday and think we will have them back when we get home." Values aren't like a comfortable shirt that you wear for lounging but never to work. Ben and Jerry's successful company reflected their values of social responsibility. They understood that participation in an enterprise feels more meaningful and satisfying when it shares one's core values. Here, you'll determine your own values so you can more readily find careers that match them.

Values and Career Satisfaction

Do you feel as though your time at work is time taken away from your real life? If your rich Uncle Bob left you $1 million tomorrow, would you quit your job? If you answered yes to one or both questions, you probably aren't doing work that aligns with your values.

Searching for Meaning

More and more people of all ages and at all career stages are searching for meaning in their working lives. There are several reasons for this heightened search. A lifetime of guaranteed job security with one employer is a thing of the past. People are changing jobs and careers more frequently due to such factors as shifts in the global economy, downsizing, and the increased use of technology, as well as the elimination of middle management positions. Increasing numbers of workers soon come to understand the importance and necessity of managing their own careers. The act of switching from one employer to another offers you the chance to assess interests, skills, values, and other qualities and align that information with your career decisions.

Learning New Skills

Another aspect of this increased search for meaning is that it motivates people to improve and expand their marketable skills. Stagnating in one place, working with old technology, or using archaic skills can make it much harder to find new opportunities and challenges at work. People need and desire new experiences, and that need compels more workers to seek out careers where they can grow, learn, meet new challenges, and use their abilities in significant ways. That kind of work is never boring.

Following Your Spiritual Path

Spirituality and the search for meaning are increasingly seen as part of work, not separate from it. Trend-tracker Patricia Aburdene calls the focus on spirituality and its convergence with business "today's greatest megatrend." Career professionals often hear clients express a need to get more than just a paycheck out of their jobs. Author and motivator Stephen Covey offers the analogy of spending your entire life climbing a ladder only to get to the top and find out it's leaning against the wrong wall. Don't let that happen to you.

Defining Success

Finally, the definition of success is no longer as linear, clear, or obvious as it seemed previously. People want to create their own definitions of accomplishment that link their values to their work. For some, earning a huge salary may be well worth the inability to spend time with family and friends. For others, the lure of prestige may pale in comparison to the opportunity to help others who are less fortunate. Every day, people accept promotions or resign from high-powered jobs in order to pursue careers that they perceive to be more rewarding based on their own criteria. In 2006, Bill Gates announced that in 2008 he would quit his daily involvement in Microsoft to head his charitable foundation full-time. The motivating force for such people is their values and the desire to fit into a workplace where the values mesh with their own. As values coach and author Michael Henderson writes in *Finding True North* (HarperCollins), "It is our values that give us meaning in life, and meaning, in turn, provides us with strength, motivation, and willpower."

What Are Values?

For millennia, philosophers, sociologists, psychologists, and others have tried to figure out just exactly what values are. You have them; all humans do. The word comes from the Latin *valeo*, to be strong. Values can be likened to roots that keep a tree upright and anchored against the onslaught of the elements. Your values steady you against the maelstrom of everyday life. The definition of values varies, but there are some points upon which most experts seem to agree.

Values are:

- **Deeply held constraints, ideals, convictions, or standards.**

- **Lifestyle priorities.** Even among people with identical values, each person will give a value greater or lesser importance in relation to that individual's life.
- **Motivators for behavior.** You are motivated by those values you adhere to most passionately.
- **Highly subjective.** Your unique combination and prioritization of values define you as an individual. There is no one "right" set of values for everyone.
- **Ways that you react and relate to the world around you.** Psychologist Milton Rokeach calls values "ways of being."
- **Developed from your life philosophy.** This comes from culture; nation; experiences with teachers, friends, parents, and others important to you; and other environmental influences.
- **Always present, often unconscious.** They're part of who you are and color your work and nonwork actions and decisions whether you are aware of them or not.
- **Relatively stable over time.** Values may shift as your needs and perceptions change and you grow, learn, and mature. Societal events can affect values, too. An Australian study found that the priority of values such as safety and security increased markedly among workers after September 11, 2001.

Values are not:

- **Physical objects.** However, objects can come to represent our values, such as the way a treasured heirloom can represent values of family, tradition, or beauty.
- **Beliefs.** Beliefs are convictions or opinions, but values grow out of and are greatly influenced by underlying beliefs.
- **Emotions.** One's values can lend clarity to circumstances clouded by emotion and can even transform one's emotional state.
- **Behaviors, habits, or attitudes.** Values influence your behaviors and attitudes but don't predict them. When was the last time you heard someone say, "Do as I say, not as I do!" Perhaps that person was acting against her values because of a particular set of circumstances.

- **Morals or ethics.** Morals are established standards for good behavior. Ethics are agreed-upon codes of behavior. Morals, ethics, and values are interrelated and affect one another. One way to remember the difference: Morals and ethics constrain; values motivate.
- **Principles.** Principles are time-tested basic truths, rules, or standards. They can be self-imposed or adopted. The British social researcher Richard Titmuss pointed out the difference between principles and values when he wrote, "Even thieves have values. It's their lack of principles that makes them different from others."
- **Fixed in a hierarchy.** It is impossible to determine for all time and in all circumstances that being polite is more important than being forgiving or that being capable is more important than being logical.
- **Situational.** You don't just conjure up friendliness, ambition, or broad-mindedness when you need it. If these are some of your values, they pertain to all aspects of your life, not just at work or at home.
- **Derived from what you're told.** As noted previously, values emerge from how others behave toward you. No one can tell you to love or respect him or her. Where values are concerned, actions do speak louder than words.

Values are abstract ideas, and as such it's sometimes easier to recognize them when they're absent, like health or respect. Values are often confused with many things with which they are related, so it helps to know what values are not.

A Short History of the Study of Values

Twenty-four hundred years ago, the philosopher Plato searched for the ideal values by which he thought the citizens of Greece should live. He came up with some good ones, too, including courage, justice, happiness, knowledge, and truthfulness. Plato believed that the people who lived according to these values possessed character of a higher order and reaped lifestyle benefits as a result. He felt that ignoring these values led to all manner of societal evils and disharmony.

In 1931, psychologist Gordon Allport came up with a list of what he called traits, what we would now call values, easily recognized consistencies that are unique to you and define your life. Allport also devised six categories of values:

- **Theoretical** (such as truth)
- **Economic** (such as usefulness)
- **Aesthetic** (such as beauty)
- **Social** (such as love)
- **Political** (such as power)
- **Religious** (such as unity)

He was among the first to study values more as concrete links to ordinary life and less as concepts tied to virtuous living.

Other researchers in the 1930s were interested in finding out how a person's values affected fulfillment, success, and happiness. Some of them developed new ways to classify values, while others sought to come up with a definitive list. In 1935, *The Journal of Abnormal Psychology* published A. Hunt's list of seventy-six values, which included Plato's courage as well as others that would make a Boy Scout proud: cheerfulness, cleanliness, initiative, good sportsmanship, dependability, and such intangibles as effectiveness. In the 1950s, W. A. Scott came up with eighteen "moral values" that overlapped some of Hunt's but also included righteousness, intelligence, loyalty, respect for authority, and humility.

Instrumental and Terminal Values

In his book, *The Nature of Human Values* (Free Press), Milton Rokeach identified a concept of values as "an enduring belief that a specific mode of conduct . . . is personally and socially preferable to alternative modes." He published his own list of eighteen "instrumental" values and eighteen "terminal" values. Instrumental values help you determine how you behave. They include capable, self-controlled, logical, independent, and forgiving. Terminal values are idealized end-states that you hope to achieve in your life or that you hope will come to characterize the world around you. They include equality, salvation, wisdom, a world of beauty, an exciting life, and a comfortable life. Still a popular instrument, the Rokeach Value Survey asks a person to rank the relative importance of each value in the lists of terminal and instrumental values.

Values and Fulfillment

In the 1960s, Abraham Maslow was one of the first to recognize the integral role of values in a person's inner decision-making process, particularly in decisions regarding self-actualization, or developing one's full potential. Maslow asserted that good values motivate a person to get where he or she wants to go. While some people feel that core values are immutable and enduring throughout one's life, Maslow felt that people could choose the values by which they acted and that some values produced more positive benefits than others. He observed that self-actualizing individuals had more confidence, joy, and zest and were what he termed "healthy" humans.

Universal Values

More recently, researchers have tried to reach consensus on the most important or universal values. In the 1980s, Darrell Franken started with all of the lists generated by his predecessors and added key values gleaned from seven major religions and disparate organizations and disciplines such as Rotary, Tae Kwon Do, and Alcoholics Anonymous. The result was a synthesis of thirty-one values, many of them recognizable from the earlier lists, but also including others such as optimism, imagination, thrift, harmony, thankfulness, and humility. The value rated number one, meaning it appeared most frequently among all the sources Franken consulted, was compassion.

Finding True North includes an inventory of 125 values built from thirty years' work by Henderson's colleagues in Brazil, Australia, and elsewhere. His list includes a few newly coined words, such as *ecority*, to capture values that previously lacked specific words. (Henderson defines ecority as "the personal, organizational, or conceptual influence to enable persons to take authority for the created order of the world and to enhance its beauty and balance through creative technology in ways that have worldwide influence.")

Optimum Values

Since 1998, Martin E. P. Seligman, Mihaly Csikszentimihalyi, and others have been promoting research in a field they call positive psychology. They want to find out what values shape a person's destiny, what it is that makes some people, but not others, function well, achieve success, and become personally fulfilled. They have continued the search for universal values, which they call "signature human strengths," those core values that are consistent across cultures and time. They say people can be taught kindness and generosity. Signature strengths arise from something deeper. Their six main values are wisdom, courage, humanity, justice, temperance, and transcendence. Each can mean something different to different people and under different circumstances. The fact that some of Plato's values from 2,500 years ago are still on the list argues in favor of at least some universal human values.

Why Values Matter

Career professionals do agree that values are primary motivators for human behavior. Psychologists say that you will be happier, healthier, and, in general, better off when your motivation comes from your own well-defined set of core values.

How Your Values Affect Your Life

When you are clear about your value priorities, other things become more clear-cut. The lifestyle you desire is defined in terms of those core values, and with that lifestyle comes a set of goals, needs, wants, and aspirations. Your values then color the way you address each of those goals, needs, wants, and aspirations. If you value friendship highly, you will do anything within your power to make and keep your friends. If helpfulness is your primary value, then it isn't difficult to imagine that your lifestyle includes opportunities for teaching, volunteering, nursing, or mentoring. If autonomy is your highest priority, then you will make decisions that give you the independence you need. If fun is your primary value, then time and money that might be spent otherwise will go into having fun. Of course, adopting a lifestyle based on fun could cause you stress, financial difficulties, and even illness. Not all values produce positive consequences all of the time.

Core values are particularly indispensable in times of crisis. The upheaval that comes from events that are out of your control, such as being laid off from your job, forces you to examine your deepest needs. Your values provide the steadying foundation upon which to build a new, meaningful career. Identifying your most important values will point you in your right direction.

Values and Career Choices

Your values influence your choices with regard to occupation, employer, corporate culture, family, and community involvement. No doubt you can now see the advantages of linking your career to your core values. Milton Rokeach wrote, "The fit between the individual and various components of the individual's environment is not always perfect." If you ignore your values for the sake of a job, you run the risk of creating a disconnect that could potentially sabotage your own success. You may lose interest in your work, grow dissatisfied or angry, or stop caring about the organization altogether. The result is that you and your employer both lose. If your values closely match those of your organization, you will be perceived as contributing a great deal, while attaining your personal goals. The stage is set for satisfaction and success on both your parts.

Aligning your career with your values can help you:

- Lower stress
- Raise morale
- Increase productivity
- Gain cooperation
- Enhance understanding
- Learn respect
- Feel fulfilled
- Grow as a person
- Prioritize tasks

With your values prioritized, you will see advantages when it comes to making decisions, too. Roy Disney once said, "It's not hard to make decisions when you know what your values are." All jobs entail tradeoffs. Do you crave more prestige, higher pay, a chance to help others, increased job security, more variety, increased risk, and more independence? You may want them all, but the chances are good that you can't have them all. You have to make trade-offs. The way to do that is by assessing each desire in light of your core values. Your values won't change, but you will decide which ones are more important to you right now in your present circumstances. Ultimately, values provide guidelines for answering the question: "What is most important to me?" When it comes to your career, there is no question more important than that.

Values Test

Clarifying your personal values is a critical step toward understanding your own definition of success, finding new career options, evaluating specific organizations to work in, and understanding how to change your current work situation to make it more meaningful and fulfilling. The process gives you a deeper sense of what makes your life meaningful and helps you see how certain career decisions affect your life. Knowing your values makes you resilient. Just like that storm-lashed tree with deep roots, a person with strong core values doesn't bend every which way the workplace wind blows. This test is designed to help you identify your core values and craft a work life that is consistent with them.

While it's difficult to separate your work life from your whole life, think only of your work life when choosing values for this test, since your career is what you're considering now. You may realize that you crave autonomy and variety in your work life but that those values aren't as high a priority in your personal life. Later you may find it helpful to use this test to prioritize your nonwork-related values, too.

Values are highly individual; therefore, there are purposely no definitions given for the words following. Each word means something different to different people. Reflect on what each value word means to you. Think about whether or not you want that particular value to influence your current and/or future decisions regarding your work. Photocopy the test pages before you begin so you can retake the test in the future. Circle your ten most important values.

Accomplishment	Family	Nature
Adventure	Friendship	Obligation
Affiliation	Fun	Pleasure
Artistic Expression	Harmony	Predictability
Authority	Health	Recognition
Autonomy	Helpfulness	Respect
Balance	High Earnings	Responsibility
Beauty	Honesty	Risk-Taking
Challenge	Humility	Self-Discipline
Community	Independence	Self-Restraint
Competence	Influence	Service
Competition	Integrity	Spirituality
Contribution	Justice	Stability
Control	Knowledge	Structure
Cooperation	Leadership	Status
Creativity	Learning	Team Work
Curiosity	Love	Time Freedom
Diversity	Loyalty	Trust
Duty	Meaning	Variety
Faith	Moderation	Wisdom

Adapted with permission from Mark Guterman and Terry Karp of the Bay Area Career Center, San Francisco, CA (*www.bayareacareercenter.com*).

Defining Your Values

Write your top ten values in the following spaces. Then write a few words or a phrase about what that value means to you. Be as specific as you can. If you want to list a value that is not included in the list, record it on this page and write a definition that's meaningful to you. As you write your definitions, also answer the following questions.

1. Is this value critical to my job satisfaction? (Circle the C for Critical or NC for Not Critical next to each value word.)
2. Is this value present in my current work situation? (Circle P for Present or NP for Not Present next to each value word.)

Pay particular attention to any values that you labeled "Critical" and "Not Present" in your current work situation. Write all the value words you marked "Critical" on the chart on page 178.

Value 1	_____	C / NC	P / NP
Value 2	_____	C / NC	P / NP
Value 3	_____	C / NC	P / NP
Value 4	_____	C / NC	P / NP
Value 5	_____	C / NC	P / NP
Value 6	_____	C / NC	P / NP
Value 7	_____	C / NC	P / NP
Value 8	_____	C / NC	P / NP
Value 9	_____	C / NC	P / NP
Value 10	_____	C / NC	P / NP

Mapping Your Values

In the following ValueSearch™ Map, there are eight value categories defined and connected to a cluster of values. Read the definitions for each category.

Most people can categorize their specific values as indicated on the Map. However, your personal experience or value definitions may reflect a different category than those shown here. Balance, spirituality, and family are examples of values people often move to different categories. Highlight or circle each of your top ten values in the suggested categories only if the category represents your personal definition of the value. If another category feels like a better fit, simply write the value word in that category.

Now see if your values cluster in one or more categories. If they do not cluster, go back to the value word list and select your next ten most important values. Categorize those values on the Map.

ValueSearch™ Map

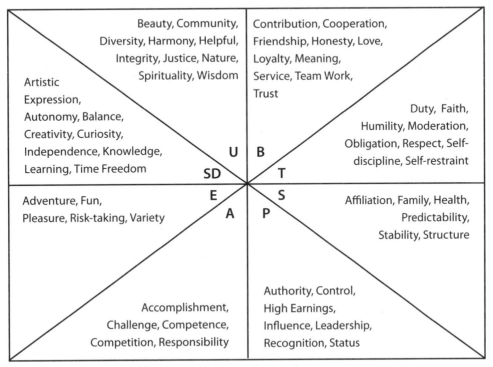

- **Universality (U):** Understanding, appreciation, tolerance, and protection for the welfare of people and nature.
- **Benevolence (B):** Concern for the protection and enhancement of the welfare of people with whom one is in frequent contact.
- **Tradition (T):** Respect, commitment, and acceptance of the customs and ideas that one's culture or religion expects of individuals.
- **Security (S):** Desire for safety, harmony, and stability of society, relationships, and self.
- **Power (P):** Attainment of social status, prestige, influence, authority, or leadership of people and resources.
- **Excitement (E):** Seeks pleasure or sensuous gratification. Enjoys
- **Achievement (A):** Desire for personal success or accomplishments; need to demonstrate competence in everday life
- **Self-Direction (SD):** Pursues independent thought or action. Enjoys the ability to choose, create, and explore.

ValueSearch™ Model

Values, as you now realize, strongly influence your behavior, decisions, and actions. This process of defining and mapping your values can help you better understand how your values can influence and motivate your career decisions. A simpler way to understand your values is to see the Map as being composed of four value types (see the following). Write the word for the value type that most closely resembles you on the chart on page 178.

Self-Transcendence

	Universality	Benevolence	
Openness to Change	Self-Direction	Tradition	**Conformity**
	Excitement	Security	
	Achievement	Power	

Self-Enhancement

Outer Layer Definitions:

Self-Transcendence: Combines values of universality and benevolence, which motivate people to transcend selfish concerns in order to promote the welfare of others and nature. Possible careers include nonprofit organizations, helping professions, or management positions enabling you to mentor or coach others. Working on a well-functioning project team or for a company or department with a compatible organizational culture may also satisfy these values.

Openness to Change: Combines values of self-direction and excitement, indicating a desire by individuals to follow their own intellectual and emotional interests in unpredictable and uncertain directions. Many creative people fall within this category, as well as those who value intellectual challenge and stimulation. Flexibility may be an important factor for your career satisfaction. You may find it appealing to have some degree of variety or unpredictability in your life.

Conformity: Combines values of tradition and security, leading to a desire to preserve the status quo and the predictability this provides in relationships with other people, institutions, and traditions. If your values cluster in this area, stability may be quite important to you. You also may need to have a clear sense of your job's required tasks and responsibilities.

Self-Enhancement: Combines values of achievement and power by indicating a desire of individuals to enhance their own personal interests. If your values fall into this category, you may need to perform a job that is quite challenging or work where you can feel as if you are accomplishing something. Also, your career satisfaction may be dependent on the opportunity for increasing levels of responsibility and/or power.

Connecting Your Values to Your Work

The purpose of this exercise is to help you evaluate how well your values are integrated into your work situation right now. It also provides you with an opportunity to consider what action steps you could take to align your career more closely with your most important values.

1. Which of your highest priority values are being realized in your current work situation?

   _____

   _____

   _____

2. Which of your highest priority values are lacking in your current work situation?

   _____

   _____

   _____

Write these values on page 178.

Using Your Results

Now that you've identified those values that are of critical importance to your career satisfaction, you can begin to find ways to include them into your work life.

Incorporate Core Values into Your Current Job

You may not be in a position to change the way work is done in your job or to change jobs, but there are other ways you can meld your highest priority values with your situation. If health is one of your values, try organizing a lunch-hour walking group, getting the junk-food machines removed from the lunchroom, or suggesting to your human resources department that it hold a health fair. If you crave more variety, do something as simple as parking on a different side of the complex so you have to walk through other parts of the building. If you have free moments, volunteer to help out in another department now and then. One museum gives its employees time off in exchange for time spent on work-related activities that aren't part of their normal jobs. For example, when an exhibit designer helps stuff gift bags for a fund-raising event sponsored by the development department, the department gets free labor and the designer learns more about fund-raising events while interacting with people he may not work with on a day-to-day basis.

Research Workplace Values of Places You'd Like to Work

As you conduct informational interviews or even interview for a new job, try to craft your questions in such a way that the answers will help you determine if your core values mesh with those of your workplace culture. For instance, if you're researching careers in real estate, do the core values of each firm include competition or teamwork, service or structure? Ask job interviewers questions such as: "What words would you use to describe the culture of this organization?" "How would you describe the work style of the group I'd be part of?" For some corporations, creativity and profit come before anything else; for others, social responsibility and collaboration may be high on their value list. Knowing the answers will guide you as you decide whether or not such a workplace would be a good fit for you.

Armed with new information about your priority values, you can now direct your time, energy, and resources into finding careers that you think best fit them. The hardest part will be resisting all of the work and social pressures that can derail you from what you have decided is really important to you. Just remember the words of that astute observer of humanity, Shakespeare: "To thine own self be true." Now you will add to your self-assessment by looking at your skills and how they impact your career.

Chapter 3
Skills and Your Career

You already have many skills, even some of which you may be unaware. You might need to brush up on others, or you may want to acquire new ones. If you have your heart set on a particular career, you can probably master the necessary skills. Learning, improving, and maintaining skills are important because they are what keep you engaged and even passionate about your work. It's important to identify those skills that you really want to use in your career.

Who Needs Skills?

Everyone needs skills. No matter what kind of career you have or want, there are skills that you need to have in order to excel. Skills are those things that you do, such as analyze, listen, add, or write. Some skills are developed through schooling, training, various jobs you have held in the past, and even hobbies and other recreational pastimes. Other skills may just come naturally to you, like telling a story.

Try to think about activities you enjoy and do well, those things you can do without thinking or that engross you to the point that you don't notice the passage of time. Perhaps you loved campaigning for student body president back in high school. Speaking extemporaneously, planning a strategy, and persuading people to vote for you gave you more satisfaction than any term paper or soccer game ever did. Perhaps the thing you liked best about your last job was the vacation away from it when you did construction on your house, hammering nails, mixing concrete, and making something tangible with your hands. Finding a career that lets you use some or all of your favorite skills will greatly enhance your chances for satisfaction and success. You will enjoy your work because it will feel more like sailing with the wind rather than rowing against it. Values, passion, and desire count for a lot, but in order to excel at a career, you have to prepare yourself with the necessary skills.

Who Has Skills?

You do. You probably think you have a pretty good handle on what skills you possess. After all, you've spent many hours learning how to do whatever it is you do, whether it's programming computers, building rocking chairs, designing gardens, or teaching second grade. You have no doubt spent even more time performing the specific tasks related to that career. You already know what your skills are, right? Maybe. Believe it or not, one expert estimates that every person has about 700 different skills at his or her disposal.

Imagine you're a respiratory therapist (or thinking of becoming one). It goes without saying that you need to have a firm grounding in the medical information and techniques related to your specialty. It's pretty obvious, too, that you should have good interpersonal skills in order to assess and treat patients. But did you realize that respiratory therapists also use good active listening skills to pay close attention to what people say and understand them, critical thinking skills to identify the strengths and weaknesses of alternatives, and monitoring skills to assess the status of patients in order to take appropriate actions? All of these are recognized skills used in most working situations to a greater or lesser degree, depending on the job. They are all skills you possess to some extent, and they are all skills you can learn or improve.

Even if you have never held paid employment before, you have some of the skills required and valued in the workplace. A stay-at-home parent's day is filled with food planning and preparation, chauffeuring, and home maintenance, as well as listening, negotiating, instructing, coordinating, monitoring, money management, and scheduling. As Abraham Zoleznik wrote in his book *In Support of Families*, "Being a parent is a form of leadership." But there are also specific skills that you need to acquire, hone, and maintain in order to excel at any specific career you wish to pursue.

What Are Skills?

There are lots of different ways to categorize skills. The U.S. Department of Labor separates them as skills with ideas, skills with people, and skills with things. Some career specialists divide work-related skills into other general categories, such as those that follow. Any career is going to require some combination of these types.

Basic Work Skills

There are three certainties in life: death, taxes, and change. The workplace of the twenty-first century is a rapidly changing environment. The work skills required today bear scant resemblance to those needed even fifty years ago, in the days before personal computers, the Internet, and photocopiers. Today's basic skills for any job, from sales clerk to CEO, programmer to playwright, are varied and many faceted. These basic skills are the ones employers seek most often in their employees.

- **Communication:** the ability to convey information effectively, convincingly, and clearly
- **Reading:** the ability to comprehend and interpret information, signs, symbols, documents, instructions, policies, diagrams
- **Writing:** the ability to compose and understand correct standard English in forms, documents, letters, reports, and other printed matter
- **Thinking:** the ability to use logic and reasoning to solve problems, identify the strengths and weaknesses in alternative solutions, brainstorm, and be creative
- **Mathematics:** the ability to produce and understand financial documents, budgets, tables, graphs, measurements
- **Learning Strategies:** the ability to select and use new information and understand its implications to your field
- **Time Management:** the ability to organize and perform tasks effectively and efficiently

Technical Skills

These include skills that are specific to a particular career and can include anything from using a certain piece of equipment to managing and scheduling a complicated project. Perhaps last year's Earth Day inspired you to become an environmental scientist. You'll need more than a deep and abiding love for the planet. Depending on the specialty area you choose, you will need many skills in, for example, scientific reasoning and methods and using all sorts of equipment, from anemometers and pH meters to air samplers, flowmeters, and radon detectors. You might need to test soil, take core samples, monitor groundwater, or measure toxic mold. You may need to know how to use a global positioning system, aerosol spectrometer, noise dosimeter, and ionization chamber. Back in your office you will need to be able to understand the literature in your field and be proficient in the use of a desktop computer, which is probably loaded with software for analyzing data, creating maps, managing databases, tracking emissions, compiling spreadsheets, managing projects, and writing presentations.

Interpersonal Skills

Every job means interacting with other people and this requires some proficiency in interpersonal skills. Some careers require a lot more than others. Remember that career as an environmental scientist that you desire so passionately? It involves more than hugging trees and communing with chipmunks. You are going to need to be able to listen actively to colleagues and give them your full attention, understand what they say, and ask appropriate questions. You might need to persuade them to change their minds or behavior. You'll want to be aware of others' reactions and understand why they react the way they do. You will need to gather data from others to make sure your work meets their requirements or needs. As you are coordinating your actions with those of the people you work with, you will need to be able to communicate information through conversations, presentations, or written reports. If you manage a project or a department, you will need to know how to lead and motivate people effectively in order to get the results you want while keeping harmony in the workplace.

But most skills you can learn. Like a box full of specialized tools, you can add to them, sharpen them, and take them with you from job to job. Research shows that people derive satisfaction from their career when they have the necessary skills and abilities to perform well.

Skills Employers Demand Most

In a 2005 survey conducted by the National Association of Colleges and Employers (NACE), employers rated the most desired employee skills on a scale of 1 to 5, with 5 being "extremely important." Here are the skills most in demand.

Skill	Rating (1–5)
Communication	4.7
Teamwork	4.6
Analytical	4.4
Interpersonal	4.4
Computer	4.3
Organizational	4.1
Leadership	4.0

How do you measure up in these areas? You'll have a chance to find out when you take the following test.

Who Lacks Skills?

Recent surveys of high school students, college students, college graduates, job seekers, and employers reveal some discouraging statistics. A study conducted by Peter D. Hart Research Associates for Achieve, Inc. (February 2005) found that 49 percent of high school graduates who didn't go on to college felt unprepared in the skills, abilities, and work habits expected of them in the workforce. Of those who went right from high school to jobs, 84 percent felt they needed more education or training to fulfill their career expectations. Their potential employers agreed with them, saying that 39 percent of high school students were unprepared for entry-level jobs and 45 percent didn't have the skills needed to advance beyond entry level.

As for employees, in 2001, the American Management Association published its findings that 34.1 percent of job applicants tested in basic skills (ability to read instructions, write reports, and do arithmetic) lacked sufficient skills for the positions they sought. An article in *Computerworld* (August 2003) listed a lack of communication skills among the shortcomings in IT workers and added troubleshooting, project management, and business skills to the list. A University of Phoenix survey (January 2005) found that 65 percent of employers worried about a shortage of skilled workers in the fastest growing industries (health care, education, business, computer systems, sales).

In one localized example, the Chamber of Commerce of Grand Rapids, Michigan, conducted a job skills survey of over 400 regional employers in 2004. They were asked to list the skills found lacking in entry-level employees; the top deficits included thinking, work efficiency, and interpersonal skills. A 2006 labor forum in Wisconsin identified a lack of basic skills in reading, writing, and mathematics as a worsening trend in the job market.

The problem isn't confined to the United States. A January 2006 survey conducted by Manpower, Inc. polled 33,000 employers across twenty-three countries. The data found that 40 percent expressed difficulty in filling positions due to a lack of suitable talent. The numbers are higher for Mexico (78 percent), Canada (66 percent), and Japan (58 percent). The top five jobs that employers are having trouble filling in the countries surveyed are these:

1. Sales representatives
2. Engineers
3. Technicians (production/operations, engineering, maintenance)
4. Production operators
5. Skilled manual trades (carpenters, welders, plumbers)

Recent government research in the United Kingdom identified skills shortages as a "greater threat to business performance than the rising price of oil or the fragility of consumer spending." The poll found that 80 percent of British employers predicted their business would be threatened in 2006 because of a lack of skilled people to fill recruitment needs. In early 2006, the Business Council of Australia issued a report decrying the lack of communication, entrepreneurial, and problem-solving skills among that country's university graduates. Even India, where many call center and IT jobs have been outsourced from the United States, faces a huge worker shortage in the coming years due to a lack of skills and experience in the workforce, according to a McKinsey and Company report.

Skills Test

This test will help you think about the skills you have, those you enjoy using the most, and those you enjoy the least. It will also help you identify skills you would like to develop. Identifying your skills can help you see which jobs are right for you. A good fit between skills and career will keep your motivation high, your outlook energetic, and your performance optimum. Use your results to help you identify new career fields, take advantage of opportunities with your current employer, or even plan for retirement.

The skills are grouped into four work styles. Rate each skill "do not like using," "neutral," or "enjoy using." You may find that you have a preference for skills in just one or perhaps two of the style categories. List the skills you rated as "enjoy using" on the chart on page 180. You might also make a separate list of those skills you rated with a 1. Knowing these will help you avoid careers that require them.

The Skilled Organizer

My natural style is orderly and efficient. I use logical analysis to solve problems and to make decisions. I like to organize and plan my projects or programs. I need a work environment that is steady and guided by a well-constructed strategic plan. I am attracted to leaders who define clear objectives and deliver on their promises.

do not like using	neutral	enjoy using	
❑	❑	❑	**Budget:** Plan for expenditures or allocation of resources.
❑	❑	❑	**Implement Procedures:** Carry out or put into effect procedures or protocols.
❑	❑	❑	**Calculate/Compute:** Count or figure amounts. Execute a mathematical process.
❑	❑	❑	**Edit Reports/Stories:** Prepare reports or stories for presentation or publication.
❑	❑	❑	**Estimate Costs:** Make approximate calculations or preliminary assessments of cost.
❑	❑	❑	**Control Inventory:** Purchase and track supplies, goods, or merchandise.
❑	❑	❑	**Organize Projects:** Plan, arrange, or systematize tasks to meet specified goals.
❑	❑	❑	**Coordinate Events:** Plan and organize event details such as time, facilities, and agendas.
❑	❑	❑	**Remember Details:** Memorize and recall particulars.

do not like using	neutral	enjoy using	
❑	❑	❑	**Use Space Efficiently:** Arrange physical elements for greatest utility or ease of movement.
❑	❑	❑	**Categorize:** Classify or arrange into categories.
❑	❑	❑	**Map Routes:** Plan and delineate paths or courses of travel or transportation.
❑	❑	❑	**Monitor Quality:** Oversee process to ensure standards are met.
❑	❑	❑	**Retain Facts:** Hold and maintain knowledge of demonstrable truths.
❑	❑	❑	**Appraise:** Evaluate the value of something.
❑	❑	❑	**Audit:** Examine records or accounts for accuracy.

The Skilled Liberator

My natural style is action-oriented and adaptive. I enjoy challenges and am open to change. I see adventures and new opportunities. I am a trouble-shooter in my work and recreation. I like work that is exciting. I enjoy being outdoors and/or having a high degree of mobility in my work.

do not like using	neutral	enjoy using	
❑	❑	❑	**Repair:** Fix or restore something to working condition after damage.
❑	❑	❑	**Troubleshoot:** Identify sources of trouble or causes of malfunction.
❑	❑	❑	**Use Tools:** Employ or manipulate handheld implements.
❑	❑	❑	**Draft:** Create a visual representation of a plan for construction or manufacture.

do not like using	neutral	enjoy using	
❏	❏	❏	**Risk:** Undertake high-risk projects or tasks to increase profits or save lives.
❏	❏	❏	**Paint:** Apply coating or pigments for artistic expression or utility.
❏	❏	❏	**Make Crafts:** Create artistic objects with one's hands.
❏	❏	❏	**Use Physical Dexterity:** Demonstrate skill and coordination in use of body.
❏	❏	❏	**Utilize Technology:** Solve problems with computer software, mechanical devices, or electronics.
❏	❏	❏	**Add Humor and Fun:** Contribute a funny or amusing element to environment or process.
❏	❏	❏	**Improvise:** Create spontaneously or make do with available resources.
❏	❏	❏	**Mobilize:** Rally, prepare, and coordinate others, especially in response to crisis.
❏	❏	❏	**Market Products/Services:** Identify target consumers and develop strategies to sell products/services to them.
❏	❏	❏	**Negotiate:** Use persuasive skills to come to terms or reach agreement.
❏	❏	❏	**Prepare Food:** Assemble ingredients and create appealing meals.
❏	❏	❏	**Design Landscapes:** Conceptualize planting arrangements to meet functional and decorative goals.

The Skilled Facilitator

My natural style is interpersonal and collaborative. I am attracted to a team-oriented, democratic environment. I value authenticity, positive interaction, and harmony. I work best with leaders who communicate well and provide reinforcement. I care about employee morale and motivation. I am sensitive to the work atmosphere and feel drained by conflict.

do not like using	neutral	enjoy using	
☐	☐	☐	**Collaborate:** Work together with others in a joint effort.
☐	☐	☐	**Listen:** Tune in or pay attention in an effort to hear and understand.
☐	☐	☐	**Counsel:** Exchange opinions and ideas and/or give guidance.
☐	☐	☐	**Coach:** Provide instruction and encouragement.
☐	☐	☐	**Motivate Employees:** Provide incentive and generate excitement to achieve goals.
☐	☐	☐	**Entertain Guests:** Extend hospitality toward visitors.
☐	☐	☐	**Interview:** Direct questions or conversation to elicit facts, viewpoints, or statements.
☐	☐	☐	**Inspire:** Arouse emotions and stimulate to creativity or action.
☐	☐	☐	**Design Interiors:** Conceptualize arrangement and decoration of work or living spaces.
☐	☐	☐	**Lead Teams:** Guide or direct work of organized groups.
☐	☐	☐	**Serve Customers:** Assess needs and provide appropriate goods and services.
☐	☐	☐	**Speak in Public:** Address groups of people in a public setting.
☐	☐	☐	**Conduct Therapy:** Attend to emotional needs. Provide treatment for illness or disability.
☐	☐	☐	**Teach/Instruct:** Impart knowledge or skill through presentation, example, or experience.
☐	☐	☐	**Heal:** Restore to health or soundness; cure.
☐	☐	☐	**Use Color:** Conceptualize the use of and apply pigment for creative expression.

The Skilled Innovator

My natural style is analytical and systematic. I am a complex thinker, attracted to concepts and innovative solutions. I enjoy seeing the relationships between various ideas and drawing logical conclusions. I am a researcher and knowledge seeker. I bring vision to projects and will look at the long-term implications.

do not like using	neutral	enjoy using	
☐	☐	☐	**Consult:** Assess client needs and give expert advice as a professional.
☐	☐	☐	**Visualize/Forecast:** Form a mental image and anticipate events or conditions.
☐	☐	☐	**Plan Long-Range:** Formulate a scheme or program to achieve long-term goals.
☐	☐	☐	**Design Systems:** Conceptualize methods or procedures for operations or processes.
☐	☐	☐	**Investigate:** Make detailed inquiry to examine cause and effect.
☐	☐	☐	**Research:** Investigate or study using books, interviews, or the Internet.
☐	☐	☐	**Brainstorm:** Generate ideas and explore alternatives and other options.
☐	☐	☐	**Analyze:** Examine methodically and thoroughly.
☐	☐	☐	**Invest Finances:** Commit money or capital for profit gain.
☐	☐	☐	**Manage Projects:** Oversee organization and execution of tasks to achieve goals.
☐	☐	☐	**Advise:** Use knowledge and expertise to make suggestions or recommendations.
☐	☐	☐	**Use Logic:** Employ reasoning and rational thought processes.
☐	☐	☐	**Strategize:** Develop a comprehensive plan of action.

do not like using	neutral	enjoy using	
❑	❑	❑	**Demonstrate Confidence:** Exhibit belief in oneself and one's capabilities or expertise.
❑	❑	❑	**Explore New Concepts:** Express openness and inquire about new or unfamiliar ideas.
❑	❑	❑	**Invent:** Use imagination and ingenuity to conceptualize or create something new.

Add your checked items in each category. Write the skill style or styles that best describe you on the chart on page 178.

This exercise is adapted, with permission, from the online Elevations™ assessment found at *www .ElevateYourCareer.com*, published by Scully Career Associates, Inc. Patent pending.

Using Your Results

Your completed list of highly enjoyed skills is a reflection of your own inner wisdom and life experiences. Knowing your skills will help you articulate them to potential employers—and employers are very interested in what you can do and have done. When you find a career that uses the skills you do well, you will enhance your self-esteem and become more confident. Here are some ways to apply what you've learned from this test.

Match Your Skills to a Career

Now that you've identified your best skills, investigate the careers that use them. A good online resource is *www.careerinfonet.org,* which lets you search through hundreds of careers by the types of skills used in each one. You can then cross-check your choices by salary, education requirements, and the prospects for growth in that area over the next decade. This is particularly useful if you're thinking of becoming a telephone operator, mail clerk, or railroad signal operator. The outlook for those jobs is a nearly 40 percent decline by 2014.

Check that the career list that matches your skills also matches your interests, values, and other qualities. As you complete the tests in this book and fill out the chart on pages 178–179, you will see how all of your career qualities and qualifications coalesce into a profile of you and your career opportunities.

Avoid Burnout

When researching your career options, look for clues that your preferred skills will be supported. Notice that you may have skills that you marked as enjoying very little or not at all. These are your burnout skills. You may be adept at organizing documents into filing systems but hate the thought of spending all of your working days alone in a cubicle. Obviously, you'll want to avoid those career options that focus too much attention on these potential burnout areas.

Discuss Your Skills with Others

Get a second (or third) opinion. Ask some people who know you well to list your best skills. Their answers may surprise you and differ from the list you made yourself. Don't discount these objective opinions. Something like brainstorming may seem so effortless to you that it's more like a game than a work skill, but for those who can't think outside the box, it's an aptitude to be envied.

Talk to people doing the work that interests you and check to see how many of them use the skills you enjoy a great deal. You want to base your decisions on a realistic view of the work, not on a printed description in a want ad or Web site or what you see on a television drama. See the section on informational interviewing in Chapter 12 for some tips.

Work on Those Skills

Create a list of skills you would like to develop. You will find ideas from books; self-administered lessons; evening, online, or adult education classes; seminars; certification programs; workshops; volunteering; or mentoring. Be sure to take advantage of any skill development opportunities offered by your current employer, too.

Build a skills resume. This document is based on what you can do, not on what your responsibilities were in a particular job. It features verbs, not job titles. It's helpful to think of this resume as a marketing tool communicating the skills you offer, not a history of every job you've ever held. Don't be shy. Many people aren't comfortable promoting their own skills; to them, it feels too much like bragging. Well, if you don't toot your own horn, who will?

Practice. If you really want to improve a skill—for example, public speaking—keep at it. Join Toastmasters, give presentations to your local book club, or join an amateur acting company. You may never become the next great motivational speaker, but you will grow more comfortable in front of an audience. You may become pretty good at it. In the world of work, pretty good is something.

Skills of the Future

In a *Christian Science Monitor* article (March 2005), futurist Richard Samson opined that the great skills void of the future won't be math or manual dexterity, which are things technology can do. Humans will need to brush up on those skills that are uniquely human, such as ethical judgment, intuition, responsibility, creativity, and compassion. Witness past trends: In the nineteenth century, the percentage of Americans in agriculture shrank from 40 percent to 2, followed by a similar shrinkage in manufacturing, thanks largely to technology. Today, most employees work in service-sector jobs that can't be automated. And what with all the corporate scandals riddling the media, the idea of making ethical judgment a job requirement doesn't sound too crazy.

Daniel H. Pink outlines another way to look at future skills in his book *A Whole New Mind* (Riverhead Books). Forget assemblers and number crunchers. Again, these are jobs that machines can do. Pink says the future lies with "creators and empathizers, pattern recognizers, and meaning makers." What are the aptitudes needed for the jobs of the future?

- **Design**—not just functional, but beautiful and engaging
- **Story**—not just data, but compelling narrative
- **Symphony**—not just specialization, but synthesis
- **Empathy**—not just logic, but understanding
- **Play**—not just seriousness, but lightheartedness
- **Meaning**—not just more, but purpose

Above all, don't be afraid to try, learn from your mistakes, and improve your skills, whatever they may be.

Chapter 4

Interests and Your Career

Humorist Mark Twain got it right when he said, "The most successful people are those who do all year long what they would otherwise do on their summer vacation." Those are successful and happy people. You can build a career around virtually any subject, industry, or activity that you find interesting. Pick a career that corresponds to your interests, and just like the prolific inventor Thomas Edison, you may find it's so much fun that you'll never have to do a day's work in your life.

Do What Interests You

Maybe this scenario is familiar to you: You suffered through an excruciating job and could never quite put your finger on why you hated it so much, especially when other people seemed to revel in it. Perhaps you were stuck in an office crunching numbers when you longed to be meeting with clients, or you were told to dream up a slogan for a publicity campaign when you much preferred persuading people to donate money to a political campaign. Career-counseling professionals agree that your best career choices are ones based on your long-standing interests. Jobs in those careers are more likely to be far more fulfilling. Many successful people agree that if you're doing what you love, the money and everything else will fall into place. Finding out your particular interests—what you love to do—is the purpose of taking an interests test.

"Interests" can be any subjects, activities, or industries that you find fascinating. You may already be skilled in them or not know much about them but want to learn more. The more you know about your interests and how they fit into a predictable pattern, the more comfortable you will become with making a commitment to a career direction. Tests such as these help you see how your interests fit into the world of work. Happily, you will see that you are both unique and marketable, with qualities that employers are willing to pay for even as you take pleasure in your job.

This kind of test is both reflective and introspective. As you tap into your own understanding of yourself, you allow that information to guide your career choices. You should take this test again every few years to help track your evolving interests and monitor your career growth. A very general interest, such as liking to work with your hands, is unlikely to change during your life, but more specific interests, such as refinishing furniture or teaching elementary students, may wax or wane as you learn about new fields or get exposed to new experiences.

Think about hobbies you enjoy in your leisure time, work activities that you do or have done well, ideas and activities that are or have been important to you, appointed or elected positions you have held (which may have nothing to do with any job you have had), and any tasks you have enjoyed that were related to jobs you held in the past. Anything and everything you can think of will illuminate and inform your ultimate career decisions.

How an Interests Test Works

An instrument that assesses your interests can help you identify the theme or themes that define those interests. After you complete the test, you will begin to notice patterns in your responses. For example, understanding that you like to manage structured projects outdoors, build things, and collaborate with other people will lead you to explore different careers than if your test results indicate that you like to work alone to develop imaginative ideas while you craft images into something aesthetically pleasing. Depending on your ultimate goal, an interests test will help you:

- Organize your interests into themes or patterns
- Identify job titles to research further
- Find careers that are right for you
- Change careers
- Ascertain necessary training or further education
- Determine ways to balance your work and leisure time
- Increase your job satisfaction

What Interests Tests Don't Do

An assessment of your interests doesn't measure your aptitude, skills, or values. It won't evaluate your ability to do certain jobs or tell you whether you will ultimately be happy in a particular career. It doesn't tell you how smart you are. It also doesn't lock you into a specific type forever. As noted previously, people change and interests change.

A Short History of Interests Tests

Nearly 400 years ago, clergyman Robert Burton noted, "Birds of a feather will gather together." The field of career counseling hadn't yet been invented, but he managed to pinpoint one of its most important tenets: Individuals who work with people whose interests are similar to their own are more satisfied and productive. But it was left to later researchers to apply scientific methods to the codification of interests and discover their relationship to satisfaction in the working world.

Strong Interest Inventory

In the 1920s, military psychologist E. K. Strong, Jr. developed an assessment tool to collect information about individuals' interest in a wide range of occupations, work and leisure activities, and subjects. He then compared those preferences to the interests of people satisfactorily employed in various occupations. His work grew out of the need to assign recruits to appropriate military jobs during World War I. Strong realized that people who work in jobs that they find interesting are also more likely to find fulfillment, satisfaction, and a certain comfort level in those jobs. In 1927, Strong and Stanford University published the Strong Interest Inventory (SII). From the results, he could make general predictions about which careers would be most compatible with a person's interests.

Over the past several decades, the SII has been taken by thousands of people and revised, improved, and updated many times. It remains one of the most thoroughly researched and highly respected instruments in use today. The most widely used tests are too complex to be self-administered and scored; those are recommended for use with a career professional. However, there are simpler versions that you can take and score yourself, such as the one included here, that will give you a pretty good idea of your compatible careers.

Holland Codes

Several decades ago, psychologist Dr. John Holland also researched the factors that promoted or prevented job satisfaction. He learned that people are happiest when they work in places that let them use their abilities, feel satisfied, and avoid tasks they don't like. It seems obvious in retrospect, doesn't it? With the publication of *The Psychology of Vocational Choice* in 1966, Holland summarized his theory that people and occupations could be grouped into six basic types, identified by the letters RIASEC.

- **Realistic:** Practical, concrete, thing-oriented
- **Investigative:** Analytical, rational, introverted
- **Artistic:** Creative, independent, nonconforming
- **Social:** Cooperative, friendly, people-oriented

- **Enterprising:** Persuasive, competitive, confident
- **Conventional:** Organized, practical, conforming

Each of Dr. Holland's six codes stands for a pure, or idealized, type. You will usually see them arranged in a hexagon. The types closest to each other (for example, Realistic and Investigative or Enterprising and Conventional) have more in common with one another than types opposite from one another (such as Investigative and Enterprising). Rarely will one person personify only one type. Your vocational interests will most likely be a combination of varying degrees of several types. Some people even find that they incorporate two seemingly opposing types, such as Social and Realistic.

Your Holland Code

Consider your three-letter Holland code to be just one more piece of your self-assessment puzzle. Your code won't tell you to enter any particular occupation, but it should inspire you to explore more than one career option. Ultimately, knowing your code should spark new ideas and broaden the number of possible career opportunities that might satisfy you.

Since Dr. Holland first published his formal assessment, other people have developed many formal and informal tests that use his ideas. You can find more information about them and links to some in the appendices at the end of this book.

Interests Test

This is one of those tests that you can't study for, so don't worry about it. Think about subjects and activities you enjoy, as well as those you don't. Check all of the items that you feel describe you. Then total the checked items for each theme and write that total in the space provided. Identify your top three themes and write the three-letter code in the box provided and in the chart on page 178.

Realistic (R)

Realistic people are oriented to the present rather than the past or future. Their thought patterns are structured, and they tend to take a concrete approach to solving problems rather than rely on abstract theories. Their attitudes and values tend to the more conventional because they are tested and often reliable. Their behavior is competitive, assertive, and can be reserved. They like hands-on activities that require motor coordination, skill, and physical strength. Realistic people prefer situations that involve action rather than talking, writing, or interpersonal skills.

I am	I can	I like to
___ Practical	___ Fix, build, or repair things	___ Tinker with mechanisms
___ Athletic	___ Solve mechanical problems	___ Be outdoors
___ Straightforward	___ Play a sport	___ Be physically active
___ Mechanically inclined	___ Read blueprints or diagrams	___ Use my hands
___ Reliable	___ Operate tools, machinery, or equipment	___ Build new things
___ Persistent	___ Use physical strength to accomplish things	___ Work with objects
___ Thrifty		___ Care for animals
___ Genuine		___ Tend plants

___ = My **R** total

Investigative (I)

Investigative people are independent, analytical, and abstract. They consider themselves scholarly and intellectually self-confident, but not particularly people-oriented. They prefer to think rather than act and organize and understand rather than persuade, lead, or sell to people. They want to understand cause and effect, and they use their intelligence to figure out problems and search for facts. They are likely to be highly original, with rich vocabularies for classifying and distinguishing.

I am	I can	I like to
__ Inquisitive	__ Think abstractly	__ Explore ideas
__ Analytical	__ Analyze data	__ Use computers
__ Introverted	__ Understand scientific theories	__ Work independently
__ Scientific		__ Solve puzzles
__ Independent	__ Do complex calculations	__ Perform laboratory experiments
__ Observant	__ Conduct research	__ Read scientific or technical publications
__ Precise	__ Evaluate information	
__ Intellectual	__ Chart data on graphs	__ Study or solve problems
__ Reserved		

__ = My I total

Artistic (A)

Artistic people are interested in cultural and aesthetic areas. They value self-expression and rely on feelings and imagination. They are more likely to relate to others by indirect means through their medium. They prefer tasks that involve personal or physical skills and are more prone to expressing their emotions than others. Their focus is usually on the creation of products, ideas, or performances. They perceive themselves to have musical and/ or artistic ability. They like to work with and create new forms, designs, and patterns and use physical, human, or verbal materials for creative expression. They can be perceived as impractical.

I am

___ Creative

___ Intuitive

___ Introspective

___ Innovative

___ Original

___ Idealistic

___ Expressive

___ Emotional

___ Nonconforming

___ = My **A** total

I can

___ Draw, sculpt, or paint

___ Play a musical instrument, sing, or compose music

___ Write stories, poems, music, plays, or scripts

___ Design fashions, objects, graphics or interiors

___ Express myself creatively

___ Perform in front of an audience

I like to

___ Attend concerts, movies, theater, or art exhibitions

___ Read fiction, plays, or poetry

___ Work on crafts

___ Collect artwork

___ Read about art, literature, or music

___ Take photographs

___ Work in unstructured situations

___ Take an art course

Social (S)

Social people prefer to communicate rather than work with objects, machines, or data. They value social activities, social service, and interpersonal relationships and are very interested in other people as well as sensitive to the needs of others. They like work situations that promote learning and personal development. They are able to use their well-developed verbal and socials skills to change other people's behavior. They often seek close interpersonal relationships and are less apt to engage in intellectual pursuits or extensive physical activity. They don't see themselves as mechanically inclined but do see themselves as understanding and popular.

I am

___ Helpful

___ Insightful

___ Outgoing

___ Understanding

___ Trustworthy

___ Generous

___ Nurturing

___ = My **S** total

I can

___ Teach or train others

___ Express myself clearly

___ Lead a group discussion

___ Counsel others

___ Mediate disputes

___ Plan and supervise an activity

___ Cooperate well with others

I like to

___ Work in groups

___ Help people with problems

___ Particpate in meetings

___ Volunteer

___ Work with young people

___ Entertain others

___ Play team sports

___ Read about psychology, sociology, or human relations

Enterprising (E)

Enterprising people are doers, not thinkers. They prefer working with people and ideas rather than things. They have good speaking abilities and tend to use their verbal skills for persuading or influencing rather than supporting or helping others. They value political and economic matters, prestige, profit, and status. They enjoy starting up and carrying out projects, particularly business ventures, and taking risks for profit. These results-oriented people like to lead others and make decisions.

I am	I can	I like to
— Self-confident	— Persuade people	— Make decisions affecting others
— Assertive	— Start projects	— Participate in politics
— Adventuresome	— Sell things or promote ideas	— Excel in leadership or sales
— Persuasive	— Give a speech	— Meet important people
— Enthusiastic	— Organize activities	— Plan activities or meetings
— Ambitious	— Run my own service or business	— Read business publications
— Talkative	— Lead a group	— Belong to groups or clubs
— Extroverted	— Supervise others	
— = My **E** total		

Conventional (C)

Conventional people prefer working with data, numbers, and detail rather than ideas. They like to work where the lines of authority are clear and prefer working within regulations, routines, and standards to working in situations where they judge things for themselves. In both work and interpersonal situations, they like structure, order, and precision rather than ambiguity and are happiest when things run smoothly and efficiently. They value prestige or status.

I am	**I can**	**I like to**
— Methodical	— Work well within a system	— Work with numbers
— Accurate	— Follow instructions	— Check paperwork or products for errors
— Careful	— Set up a record-keeping system	— Work with data
— Conscientious	— Use a computer and/or office machines	— Follow clearly defined office procedures
— Efficient	— Write effective business documents	— Be responsible for details
— Detail-oriented	— Organize office procedures	— Collect and categorize things
— Patient	— Follow a set plan	— Keep accurate records
— Perseverant		— Work in an office
— = My **C** total		

Find the three categories for which you checked the most items. Write your three-letter Holland or RIASEC code here and in the chart on page 178.

RIASEC Careers

Work environments, like people, also have a predominant type, from creative to conventional. But just as with people, there will be more than one type working in any single occupational group. A pharmaceutical company, by necessity, employs many scientists and researchers, but there are also opportunities for artists (in advertising or packaging design), lawyers, maintenance staff, office assistants, and salespeople.

The eighteenth-century British author Laurence Sterne wrote, "What a large volume of adventures may be grasped within this little span of life by him who interests his heart in everything." If your interests are myriad, you will have a hard time finding one single career that will satisfy all of them. If you focus on your most important ones for work, then extracurricular activities and hobbies can take care of the rest.

Space prohibits listing every conceivable interest or career option here. Those listed in this chapter provide some ideas to get you started. The U.S. Department of Labor publishes the *Occupational Outlook Handbook* with hundreds of job ideas. The appendices here include some more resources to help you in your search.

Now that you know your three-letter RIASEC code, look through the sample occupation list for each letter of your top three categories. Put a check mark next to the ones that look most interesting to you, and record them on the chart on page 178.

Realistic Careers (R)

Realistic people value practical, concrete things they can see and touch. They like to work with plants, animals, and real-world materials, tools, or machinery in scientific or mechanical areas rather than aesthetic or cultural ones. They like structure, clear goals, well-defined lines of authority, and straightforward tasks with observable, immediate, and tangible results. They are often found in hands-on careers in such fields as agriculture, engineering, technology, or skilled trades. They prefer working outdoors to jobs that involve working closely with others or lots of paperwork.

Agricultural inspector

Baker, cook

Carpenter

Construction inspector

Desktop publisher

Driver (truck, bus)

Electrician

Engineer

Emergency medical technician

Farmer

Firefighter

Forest and conservation worker

Freight or stock movers

Landscaper

Machinist

Maintenance worker

Mechanic

Painter

Pilot

Plumber, pipe fitter, steamfitter

Surveyor

Telecommunications line installer

Welder, cutter, solderer, brazer

Investigative Careers (I)

Investigative people prefer unstructured environments that are academic and/or involve research. They are often found in careers relating to science, mathematics, medicine, and other technical fields. Their work often involves ideas and thinking rather than people, things, or physical activity. They like tasks that entail discovering, collecting, and analyzing data or ideas. They are happiest with minimal supervision and structure and often like to work alone.

Anthropologist

Architect

Astronomer

Biologist

Botanist

Chemist

Civil engineer

Computer programmer,
software engineer, systems analyst

Coroner

Dentist

Economist

Electrical engineer

Food technician

Forensic scientist

Forester

Geoscientist

Health and safety engineer

Market research analyst

Medical laboratory technician

Meteorologist

Network administrator

Oceanographer

Optometrist

Orthodontist

Pathologist

Pharmacist

Physician, surgeon

Psychiatrist

Psychologist

Speech language pathologist

Urban planner

Veterinarian

Artistic Careers (A)

Artistic people can be found in careers that relate to music, literature, dramatic arts, and other creative fields, in work environments ranging from arts organizations, film and television production, art galleries, museums, and theaters to publishing houses or advertising organizations. They prefer unstructured, flexible environments that reward unconventional and aesthetic values, where their work can be done without having to follow set rules or procedures. Hence, they tend to be frustrated in conventionally bureaucratic organizations.

Actor

Advertising artist or manager

Animator

Artist

Choreographer

Composer

Dancer

Designer (product, fashion, floral, graphic, interior, commercial, industrial, exhibit, set)

Director (stage, film, video)

Editor

Gallery staffperson

Landscape architect

Literature teacher

Merchandise displayer, window trimmer

Museum technician

Music store staffperson

Musician, singer

Photographer

Producer

Announcer (radio, television)

Reporter

Video editor

Writer (fiction, nonfiction, poetry, scripts, screenplays, plays)

Social Careers (S)

Social people prefer activities that involve interaction with other people. They are often found in careers that take advantage of their interpersonal skills, such as teaching, community awareness, and other helping vocations such as counseling or clergy. They like to give information and discuss philosophical questions. They don't gravitate toward highly ordered or routine activities or those involving machines, materials, tools, or lots of paperwork.

Anthropologist

Audiologist

Child care provider

Clergy

Clinical psychologist

Correctional officer, security guard, bailiff

Counselor (school, career, personal, substance abuse)

Dental hygienist

Fitness trainer, aerobics instructor, coach

Home health aide

Interpreter, translator

Legal assistant

Librarian

Mail carrier

Nurse

Police officer

Psychiatric caseworker

Public health worker

Social worker

Teacher (kindergarten, elementary, middle school, secondary, remedial education, special education, adult literacy)

Therapist (physical, speech-language, recreational, occupational)

Enterprising Careers (E)

Enterprising people prefer activities that involve selling, promoting, or leading. They like competition and making things happen. They avoid tasks that require attending to details, recordkeeping, careful observation or scientific, analytical thinking, and grow impatient with routine or systematic tasks. These people can be found in careers relating to sales, supervision of others, politics, and other leadership and managerial positions in organizations or entrepreneurial situations of all sizes. They like to be rewarded with money, power, or influence.

Athlete
Attorney
Bartender
Buyer
Claims investigator, adjustor
Construction manager
Cosmetologist, barber
Criminal investigator, detective
Dispatcher
Financial planner
Flight attendant
Manufacturer's representative

Occupational therapist
Producer
Public relations executive
Sales (retail, advertising, real estate, wholesale, insurance, medical, securities)
Small-business owner
Sports promoter
Stockbroker
Telemarketer
Travel agent
Waiter or waitress

Conventional Careers (C)

Conventional people prefer structured, businesslike work environments. They are found in occupations related to accounting or business and in computational, secretarial, or clerical positions. They like maintenance or administrative tasks where they can attend to details, day-to-day operations, and bottom-line results and where the focus is on the systematic manipulation of data, information, numbers, or money rather than ideas. They fit well into large organizations but don't tend to seek leadership positions.

Accountant
Actuary
Administrative assistant
Air traffic controller
Archivist
Auditor
Bank teller
Bill collector
Bookkeeper

Cashier
Computer support
Copy editor
Court reporter
Customer service
Economist
Financial analyst
Interviewer
Library assistant, library technician

Medical transcriber

Office clerk

Proofreader

Receptionist

Respiratory therapist

Tax preparer

Teacher assistant

Using Your Results

Study the job titles that you highlighted in each category and begin to think about the following points. Don't worry if you can't make any definitive decisions right now. You are still in the process of gathering information. As you take all of the tests in this book and add the results to your chart on pages 178–179, you will develop a more comprehensive picture of the career or careers that best suit you and your circumstances.

Brainstorm More Ideas

Get together with a friend or group of friends and pick their brains for more ideas about each job. In this case, two heads (or three or four) are better than one for expanding your thinking. For example, if you highlighted flight attendant as one of your job choices, ask your friends to help you list all of the qualities of that job you can think of, such as they listen, help people, provide service, are trained in emergency procedures, get to travel the world, are friendly and comfortable talking in front of people, and so forth. In this way, you'll find other jobs that could share similar qualities, such as travel agent, therapist, or teacher.

Look for Patterns

You might be surprised to notice that all of the job titles you picked, regardless of their RIASEC category, share some common characteristics. For example, if the idea of a career as a dance therapist (A and S), newspaper editor (A), or salesperson (E) appeals to you, you can see that each of these careers involves creativity, problem-solving, and good people skills. It tells you that you would prefer a job that deals with people and ideas, whether teaching, interpreting, or selling those ideas to others.

Similarly, if the ideas you want to work with include science and history, you prefer working alone or with professional peers, and you like antiquities, you can narrow your focus to careers in archaeology or museum objects conservation.

Think of Different Ways to Work in a Field

No matter if you are scientifically minded, creative, or sociable; if food is your passion you could be a pastry chef, food chemist, diner cook, waitperson, dietician, cooking instructor, nutritionist, food stylist, food historian, home economics instructor, restaurant reviewer, caterer, television cooking show host, or writer. Novelist Diana Mott Davidson writes murder mysteries that feature a sleuthing caterer and include recipes as part of the story.

If you can't narrow down your choices to a few, it may be too early to decide definitively on a career as a police officer or copy editor. Focus instead on broader fields, such as law enforcement or publishing, rather than job titles.

Do Your Research

Write down any questions you may have, from pay scale to work environment, and then look for the answers. You may find that an intriguing job requires moving to another region or country or will take many years of preparation, training, or specialized education. Depending on your age and your current level of education or training, these factors can have a huge impact on your future choices. To suddenly decide on medical school in midlife bears close consideration for its many implications, from financial to familial, not the least of which is that it could be many years before you are happily earning a salary in that career. That's not to say you shouldn't do it, if that is your interest, but go into the experience knowing all the facts. The Internet and the library are good places to start. The appendices have lots of resources to help you in your search.

Interview some people who hold the jobs that interest you. Statistics in a book can't begin to compare with firsthand information from those employed in the field. Perhaps a friend, relative, or friend of a friend can help you. Even if you contact a stranger, most people will be happy to talk about their work to someone who is genuinely interested and asks pertinent questions.

Eliminate Some Choices

As a child you may have dreamed of becoming a circus performer, but now you understand that computer graphics—not swinging from a trapeze—is your forte. One of the most valuable aspects of an interests test is that it can help you focus your choices, which will save you time, energy, and money in the long run.

A Word about Job Titles

A job title is a succinct encapsulation of what is often a highly complex occupation. Be aware that a job title may mean one thing to you and something completely different to someone else. Make sure you know what the people actually working in those jobs call them. They're more apt to take you seriously and answer your questions if you sound as though you've done your homework

A job title is a starting point. "Forensic scientist" doesn't begin to tell you all of the training and skills people in that job need to have, such as chemistry, biology, physics, statistics, and fingerprint or handwriting analysis, to name a few. Keep foremost in your mind what interests you most and the skills you have or want to acquire. Those are more important than the title of the job. Occupations with similar titles can differ widely by industry, location, and other factors. The word "teacher" might conjure up an image of Mrs. Smith in third grade, but teaching embraces a broad range of experiences, from adult literacy in an urban setting to health care with the Peace Corps in Africa.

Don't let any preconceived notions about certain careers keep you from exploring one further. If you imagine a librarian as a meek, bespectacled "Marian-the-Librarian" type, then it might be time to visit your local university library. Today's librarians work in high-tech, dynamic environments and need to be versatile and resourceful enough to quickly find all kinds of information on an infinite array of subjects and in many different formats. Similar misconceptions abound for every type of occupation. If you circled it in the test, then something about it interests you. It will be worthwhile to find out more.

Also remember that job titles change. In the 1970s, there was no such thing as a "multimedia developer." When Walt Disney created his animated Mickey Mouse cartoons, an animator drew sketches on pieces of acetate and colored them in with paint. Today, most animators need to know not only how to draw, but also how to use sophisticated computer programs. Armed with concrete knowledge of what interests you, you may even be able to create your own job title and be the first person ever to hold it!

Chapter 5

Personality and Your Career

Perhaps you've been told that you have a "bubbly" or a "serious" personality. All of your distinctive personal traits combine to make you the person you are. They affect the friends you have, activities you enjoy, and kind of life you lead. Your personality also plays a part in determining the sort of career at which you will excel and the sort of work situations in which you will thrive. Whether you're an extrovert or an introvert, there's a career just right for you.

Who's Got Personality?

You do, and yours is unique. No one else on earth has your particular assemblage of spontaneity, modesty, humor, or insightfulness. To say someone has personality doesn't just mean someone is outrageous or flamboyant, such as former Italian Prime Minister Silvio Berlusconi or the late pianist Liberace. Even the most retiring of wallflowers has personality—albeit a shy and quiet one. The word *personality* comes from *persona*, Latin for "mask." That's telling, isn't it?

Screen legend Mae West likened personality to "glitter," and while she could boast of many assets, she declared that personality was the most important factor in the success of any actress. Psychologist Erich Fromm considered personality to be "the most important product" of man's effort—the fulfillment of his potential. Albert Camus thought one's personality continued to grow and change. In the absurdist philosopher's typically upbeat fashion he wrote, "We continue to shape our personality all our life. If we knew ourselves perfectly, we should die."

Personality pertains to human differences, but it also has a lot to do with human similarities. Few people are one clear-cut personality type, such as cheerful. It's far more likely that you fall somewhere on a continuum between cheerful and dour most of the time.

What Does Personality Have to Do with Careers?

Your personality colors how you think and how you behave. It influences how you respond to different situations and how you perceive the world, make decisions, and live your life. That particular pattern of responses, perceptions, and behaviors makes up your personality. It makes sense that anything that affects how you live your life is going to affect your career satisfaction and success. It's easy to figure out that a passive introvert would likely shrivel under the scrutiny required by a career as a politician or that a gregarious person might be a good fit for a career in sales or service. But don't let such stereotypical thinking limit your own career possibilities. The purpose of personality studies isn't to pigeonhole you or anyone else. You might be an outgoing person who happens to love working with numbers. In that case, you could still thrive in a solitary accounting job, but you would have to find other ways to feed your sociable side, such as through leisure-time activities or hobbies. If you are so reclusive that the idea of initiating cold calls makes you sweat, remember from Chapter 3 that cold calling is a skill. Such skills can be learned, and you can learn to be more comfortable doing tasks that might seem almost impossible now. If you love the career, you'll find ways to make it work.

The most important thing to remember about personality in the workplace is that people are different. Those very differences are what make life and work so varied and enjoyable. You've heard the expression "Variety is the spice of life." Would you want to live and work only around people who are exactly like you? Probably not.

Those personality differences are also the things that can make a particular working situation intolerable if you don't learn how to recognize and adjust to them. You may come to find that your boss isn't mean after all; she's just so detail-oriented that she finds your fly-by-the-seat-of-the-pants work methods disconcerting.

The more you understand about your own personality themes and those of others, the better able you will be not only to find a career that suits you, but also to understand and work with the other personalities you find there.

A Short History of the Study of Personality

For as long as there have been people, there have been attempts to classify, codify, and understand what makes them the way they are and figure out how and why they differ. Those who study personality concern themselves not only with social interactions, learning, development, behavior, and culture, but also with physiology, genetics, and pathology—in short, anything that has to do with being human.

Personality in the Past

Thousands of years ago, the astrological system developed in China divided people into twelve distinct types, each displaying some of the characteristics inherent in a particular beast, such as the wily rat, self-reliant horse, or creative goat.

The Enneagram, a popular instrument used today, is thought to have roots in 4,000-year-old Pythagorean geometry. It separates people into numbered personality categories from Reformer (1) to Peacemaker (9). Margaret Fings Keyes, in her book *Emotions and the Enneagram* (Molysdatur Publications), places its origins in the secret Sufi oral traditions of Afghanistan.

Twenty-four centuries ago, Hippocrates theorized that personality was affected by four bodily fluids, or humors: black bile, blood, yellow bile, and phlegm. About 500 years later, Galen related those humors to four temperaments: melancholic, sanguine, choleric, and phlegmatic. They all sound pretty distasteful now, until you think of them in more modern terms such as serious, impulsive, sensitive, or detached. An equal balance among the four humors represented the ideal personality.

Among the accomplishments of Theophrastus, successor to Aristotle's Peripatetic school in Athens, is his book *The Characters*. In it he briefly describes a variety of moral types, including the flatterer, the dissembler, the mean, the tactless, the garrulous, and the avaricious. Some 2,300 years later, you can probably pinpoint all of these types in your own place of employment.

In the early sixteenth century, Swiss physician Paracelsus came up with a rather playful way to describe personality as influenced by salamanders, nymphs, sylphs, or gnomes.

Psychoanalytic and Behaviorist Theories

In the early part of the twentieth century, Sigmund Freud divided the human personality into three components: id, ego, and superego. He studied how people adjusted to the world around them, and he stressed the importance of early childhood experiences in shaping the adult personality. One of his colleagues, Alfred Adler, looked at a person's inner world as a determinant of behavior and personality.

In 1926, Harvard psychologist William Marston outlined four areas of human behavior: dominance, influence, steadiness, and compliance, a theory used for army recruitment before World War II and later applied to the business world.

American behaviorist B. F. Skinner suggested that external stimuli shaped an individual's personality and that a change in one's environment would significantly change one's personality. Stanford University psychologist Albert Bandura agreed that environment influences behavior but suggested that the reverse was also true. Later he added the influence of memory, feelings, and other psychological processes to that of environment in determining one's personality.

Humanistic and Biological Approaches

In marked contrast to Theophrastus's rather grumpy assessment of human personality, and to Freud's focus on childhood, psychologist Carl Rogers took the view that human behavior is rational and man's nature is essentially positive and trustworthy. According to his theory, a single force of life—the human "actualizing tendency"—is the built-in motivation to develop one's potential to the fullest extent possible. Every person is genetically programmed as a living being to do the very best he or she can.

Brandeis psychologist Abraham Maslow created the now well-known hierarchy of human needs: physiological (food, water), safety and security, love and belonging, esteem, and self-actualization. Ultimately, Maslow said that in order to be self-actualized, all of your other needs have to be met. One psychology professor calls Maslow a pioneer in the movement that "put the person back into personality" (*www.ship.edu*).

Most biologically based approaches to personality look for the particular structure, neural pathway, transmitter, or hormone associated with a particular affect, behavior, or mental process. German-born psychologist Hans Eysenck was a pioneer in this work, studying approach and reward, inhibition and punishment, and aggression and flight as facets of human genetic inheritance. In the 1950s, William Sheldon linked physical body types (ectomorph, mesomorph, and endomorph) with personality types and theorized that one's personality emerged during development in the womb.

Types, Traits, and Temperaments

The personality theory of Harvard-trained psychologist Gordon Allport rejected both behaviorism and Freud's focus on past experiences and instead looked at personality characteristics in one's present life and emphasized the individual's uniqueness. He maintained that most human behavior is motivated by functioning in a manner expressive of the self. Allport believed that each person possessed unique personal dispositions, which he called traits, and that one's central traits represented the foundation of his or her personality. Allport thought there were between five and ten central traits.

Jungian Theory

In the 1920s, Swiss psychoanalyst Carl Jung built upon Freud and Adler's work and published his own theory of psychological types. It was Jung who suggested that human behavior could be classified by how people go about such basic functions as gathering information and making decisions based on that information. He realized that some people orient themselves to the world outside themselves (extroverts) and some people orient themselves to their inner world (introverts). He then named the cognitive processes that all people engage in—thinking, feeling, sensing, and intuiting—to come up with eight types. For Jung, personality differences are the result of preferences. They emerge early and reflect both genetic and environmental influences. As preferences, there is nothing wrong with any of them—they're just different.

The Myers-Briggs Type Indicator

Around the same time that Jung was developing his ideas in the early twentieth century, Katharine Briggs was performing her own research on personality. She later set aside her work to concentrate on Jung's ideas and published a description of his theories in the *New Republic* in the 1920s.

Katharine Briggs collaborated with her daughter, Isabel, who also developed an interest in personality types. In 1930, Isabel published a novel, *Murder Yet to Come*, with characters developed using her concepts. The women thought that eventually psychology professionals would put Jung's ideas about personality types to some practical use, but it took a world war to make it happen. Spurred on by a desire to find a way to help people find jobs that suited them, Isabel Myers Briggs conducted independent research and tried a series of questions out on friends, family, and students at her children's school until she came up with sixteen distinct personality types.

Each type was rated on a continuum between opposites, and each combination of four represented one of sixteen different personality types. Here are some very general characteristics.

Extrovert or Introvert

This relates to your source of energy—from without or within. Extroverts are talkers, doers, and multitaskers. They are approachable, sociable, and gregarious. They look to others for affirmation and like to get feedback. Extroverts are energy expenders. Introverts are more territorial and internal. They're reflective thinkers and listeners who like to collect data and reach conclusions alone after considering all the options. They like solitude and quiet. Introverts are energy conservers.

Senser or Intuiter

This relates to your information-gathering style. Sensing types like doing rather than thinking, tangible results, facts and figures, and reality rather than fantasy. They see the trees rather than the forest. Intuiting types are more future-oriented. They like word play, look for the interconnectedness between things, prefer generalities rather than specifics, and are more random and conceptual.

Thinker or Feeler

This relates to your decision-making function. Thinkers are calm, detached, objective, fair, logical, and scientific. For them, it's more important to be right than to be liked. They notice numbers rather than faces. Feelers consider others' feelings, accommodate others, empathize, prefer harmony to clarity, can take things personally, and seem wishy-washy to others.

Judger or Perceiver

This relates to the function you use most to relate to the world: information gathering or decision-making. Judgers are punctual and orderly. They schedule and plan, don't like surprises, and need closure. Judgers want decisions. One source estimates that 60 percent of the world's managers are Thinking Judgers. Perceivers are more easily distracted, have a wait-and-see attitude, like to leave things open-ended and keep options open, and think work should be fun. Perceivers offer opinions.

How the Types Interact

Just from these very brief descriptions, you can begin to see the conflicts and problems that might arise when opposite personalities are required to collaborate in a work setting. The good news is that no one is a "pure" type. You share some of these characteristics with all of the other types, which means that you all have things in common. Personality and behavior are also relative. You can seem more introverted in the company of a loud, aggressive extrovert than when surrounded by others who share your introverted characteristics.

MBTI Today

In 1944, the mother-daughter duo published the test known today as the Myers-Briggs Type Indicator® (MBTI). Translated into some thirty languages, the MBTI is still one of the most widely used instruments for understanding normal personality differences, which often cause misunderstanding in the workplace. The indicator has found uses in team building, hiring and firing, career development, problem-solving, goal setting, time management, and other areas. This instrument is published by CPP, Inc. and should be administered by a professional qualified to give and interpret it.

Keirsey Temperament Sorter

In the 1970s, Dr. David Keirsey built upon Galen's four temperaments and came up with a system using Artisans, Guardians, Rationalists, and Idealists. The Keirsey Temperament Sorter uses four scales to sort people into one of the four temperaments, as well as one of four character types within each temperament (Architects, Masterminds, Inventors, and Field Marshals).

Other Personality Tests

By the 1970s, there were over three dozen major, published personality inventories looking at over 300 behaviors, values, and personality concepts. Available in books and online, they vary in quality, accuracy, and usefulness.

Personality Test

This test draws on Jung's personality and psychological types theory as well as Keirsey's work in temperament theory. The personality theme descriptions will help you understand how you communicate and how your "Most Like Me" theme and secondary theme work together.

Read through the following traits and check those that you feel strongly describe you. Assign one point to each trait and total your scores in each of the following four categories. Note your strongest theme (or themes) on the chart on page 178. Then select four traits under each theme and record those in the space provided on your chart.

☐ Orderly	☐ Action-Oriented	☐ Interpersonal	☐ Analytical
☐ Punctual	☐ Seek Adventures	☐ Team-Oriented	☐ Systematic
☐ Responsible	☐ Enjoy Challenges	☐ Authentic	☐ Logical
☐ Goal-Oriented	☐ Enjoy Excitement	☐ Motivational	☐ Objective
☐ Reliable	☐ Resourceful	☐ Empathetic	☐ Visionary
☐ Productive	☐ Spontaneous	☐ Imaginative	☐ Informed
☐ Efficient	☐ Observant	☐ Intuitive	☐ Complex
☐ Persistent	☐ Impulsive	☐ Helpful	☐ Inventive
☐ Structured	☐ Easygoing	☐ Romantic	☐ Calm
☐ Traditional	☐ Tolerant	☐ Idealistic	☐ Precise
☐ Sensible	☐ Playful	☐ Enthusiastic	☐ Innovative
☐ Detailed	☐ Exploratory	☐ Introspective	☐ Analytical
☐ Practical	☐ Adaptive	☐ Open-Minded	☐ Skeptical
☐ Realistic	☐ Flexible	☐ Caring	☐ Demanding

Total

Organizer _____   Liberator _____   Facilitator _____   Innovator _____

This exercise is adapted with permission from an online assessment called Elevations™ found at *www. ElevateYourCareer.com* published by Scully Career Associates, Inc. Patent pending.

Of course, your personality isn't the only determining factor when choosing your most suitable career. Like the Interests Test in Chapter 4, this test won't measure your skills or aptitude for a particular career or assess your intelligence or values. But taken together, your personality, interests, values, and a host of other factors will help you zero in on your ideal work situation. Just like those birds of a feather whose interests bring them together, people of similar personality types get along, too. With the help of this test, you'll find your flock.

Organizer Personality Profile

"Work before play" is the Organizer's motto. Organizers strongly believe in being responsible. They contribute to relationships by offering clear, practical suggestions to getting things accomplished. As might be expected, they have excellent organizational skills, often enjoy solving immediate problems, and want to see bottom-line results. They are detail-oriented. They arrive on time and follow a plan. Organizers need to feel that their contributions to the enterprise are appreciated. They can get frustrated with others who don't pull their own weight. They value follow-through, dependability, punctuality, and loyalty.

Organizers are faithful, organized, stable, and prepared. They need structure. They perform best when the issues and tasks at hand are clearly defined, there are rules and directions to follow, and the goals are clear. Abstract ideas and concepts are secondary until the foundation of the project is plainly presented. They feel others should share in the responsibilities. Organizers are stressed out by disorganization, unfairness, and dishonesty, as well as instability in their home, finances, or relationships.

Organizers tend to be orderly and factual. They mentally organize information in a logical fashion and present information sequentially. They tend to talk about what has worked before and will support perspectives that are financially and logically sound. They appreciate communicating with individuals who have a straightforward, direct approach. Organizers like communication to be accurate and succinct and will get frustrated by discussions that float off track or wander into irrelevant topics. In such situations they may disengage, attempt to get things back on track, or correct the speaker. This can have the effect of breaking down the flow of communication, so the Organizer may need to reduce this tendency in the workplace.

Liberator Personality Profile

Liberators enjoy a fast-paced, dynamic work environment. They use keen observational skills and quick reactions to provide practical solutions to problems. They thrive on fun, intensity, and excitement. Liberators prefer an unstructured or spontaneous approach to project management or program development. They are often mechanically inclined and rarely read the directions before they fix something. Adaptive, they enjoy situations that change frequently. In fact, they are very good in a crisis and can be relied upon for a decisive, effective response. They prefer to be physically mobile and seek jobs that require movement. For them, meetings and long presentations can be boring. They avoid jobs full of routine and structure, preferring work they can perform independently.

Liberators encourage freedom of expression in the work environment. They spice life up by offering unplanned, dynamic approaches to daily work. They can be entertaining and engaging. They prefer hands-on, short-term training and enjoy applying what they have learned on the job.

The Liberator's communication style is direct, practical, and down-to-earth. They often use humor to lighten things up, but in serious business meetings or formal presentations, this tendency can backfire. Over time, Liberators learn how far they can push the limits without harming their credibility. Liberators enjoy a free-flowing exchange that is not restricted by time constraints or arbitrary limits. They appreciate novel approaches to subjects they perceive as boring or routine. For example, a workshop instructor who uses games, creative brainstorming, or media examples will win the Liberator's approval. On the other hand, a dull monotone speaker may lose the Liberator's interest. Variety and novelty are keys to a successful interchange with a Liberator.

Facilitator Personality Profile

Facilitators value a cooperative, democratic, team-oriented approach. They have excellent communication skills and are good at getting input from others. Facilitators are concerned with the feelings of others. They are usually open to new ideas and willing to extend deadlines or change the structure to allow for innovation. They are resourceful, imaginative problem solvers. They need to have the big picture in mind before making changes to an existing structure. Facilitators are visionary and creative, as well as flexible and open to change. They operate best with regular feedback. Facilitators are committed to harmony, integrity, ethical behavior, open communication, honesty, authenticity, cooperation, bringing out the best in others, and helping others.

Facilitators care deeply about relationships and other people. They perform best in an open, interactive, cooperative atmosphere, and they tend to turn off when conflicts arise. When they get behind something they believe in, Facilitators can be powerful motivators.

Facilitators tend to be personal and interactive. They appreciate open, honest communication. Insincerity, sarcasm, or verbal attacks will shut down the flow of communication and may cause the Facilitator to withdraw or become distant. They respond well to active listeners and individuals who provide meaningful feedback. The key for the Facilitator is being understood. They can tolerate differences of opinion as long as their own perspective is heard and considered. In fact, Facilitators have a natural flair for coaching and mediation. They can sense what a person is trying to say even when the individual isn't very clear. They can take criticism to heart, losing their objectivity. This is something they may strive to change about themselves as they mature throughout their careers.

Innovator Personality Profile

For an Innovator, the front end of the project is always the best part. Innovators enjoy developing new ideas, mastering concepts, and challenging accepted ways of thinking. Innovators are independent and curious. They enjoy working with individuals who are intellectually stimulating and high achieving. As leaders, they enjoy developing the capabilities of others. Innovators can often be perfectionists and hard drivers. They have natural visionary capabilities and like to focus on the long-term impacts of their decisions. They can get bored with routine and overly detailed tasks. They prefer working on projects that have high levels of responsibility and complexity associated with them. They value logical, rational, well-researched perspectives.

Innovators are committed to competence, learning, demonstrating self-control, and clarity of purpose. They have strong convictions and are natural nonconformists. Innovators require freedom and variety and will avoid predictable assignments.

Innovators appreciate intelligent conversations and are good at keeping the conversation lively. They prefer logic to emotion and enjoy considering a variety of perspectives. Often their goal is to learn why things work the way they do or why a particular approach was taken. They generally welcome new information and may ask many questions to explore the full breadth of a subject. The Innovator is quick to move communication to problem-solving. They enjoy applying their keen analytical skills to focusing on the best options. They respect an objective, thorough exchange that drills down to the root cause of an issue, which can intimidate or overwhelm others or appear to be an interrogation rather than an exchange. The Innovator learns to pace his or her questioning and will balance curiosity with good listening skills over time.

Using Your Results

Remember that no one exhibits a pure theme—everyone has or uses all of these attributes to a greater or lesser degree. However, you probably prefer one or two over the others. By recognizing a clear preference for one or two, you can then focus on career opportunities that align with that theme or themes.

For example, if you're an Innovator, the chances are good that you have many wide-ranging interests and find it hard to settle on just one career option. Perhaps you wish you could be like those people who seem preordained to follow a particular career, who apparently knew at birth exactly what they would do and how to go about doing it.

You should be happy that you are interested in so many things. Your life won't be dull. The good news is that your results from this test, combined with your results from the other tests in this book, will help you hone in on just the right career options for you. The tips in these chapters and in the appendices will help you focus your efforts.

Integrating Multiple Themes

It's common for people to relate strongly to two personality themes. In order to get the most satisfaction out of your career, it should integrate elements from both of your strongest themes. For example, if your strongest themes are Organizer and Facilitator, perhaps you can use community service to balance the interpersonal or helpful aspects that may be missing from your Organizer career. You can look for a career that uses both your Organizer skills and your Facilitator values, such as being a project manager at a nonprofit. All of this information will help you in your career research as well as informational and job interviews. You can prepare specific questions to ensure that your Facilitator values will be supported and then look at the job description to ensure your Organizer skills are required.

If your preferences are distributed across all four themes, you're likely to be most satisfied in a career that is highly flexible and diverse, using your analytical side at some times while putting your creativity and spontaneity to work at others. Look at the traits listed in all the themes to find the ones that describe you and how you like to work. A career that makes use of these will allow you to express your varied interests and use the full range of your talents. In the long run, this will stave off boredom, dissatisfaction, or burnout.

Take Note of Your Traits

Look back at the four traits you listed under each theme in your chart. You may find these traits a useful way to describe yourself in job interviews or in workplace meetings. For example, complete the phrase, "I work best when . . . ." Your answer may be something like "processes are structured" or "I am given lots of responsibility" or "I and my coworkers stay open-minded." Just knowing these things about yourself—and about the people you work with—will help you interact more efficiently and cooperatively despite your differences.

Chapter 6

Work Environment and Your Career

Your career suits your values, skills, interests, and personality. You like your coworkers and the work you do but find it hard to get motivated in the morning. There's something standing between you and complete career nirvana. Is it the cramped cubicle? The lack of natural light? The chair that gives you a backache or the fact that you get only five days of vacation? Work environment can be as important to career satisfaction as the company for which you work. Now you'll figure out the environment that's best for you.

Find the Environment That Suits You

How, when, and where you work can be just as important as the work you do. You spend about half your waking adulthood in your work environment. It makes sense that you would come to see it as an extension of yourself and as a tangible symbol of your career aspirations and accomplishments. If it came down to it, most people would choose a supportive boss who truly values their contributions rather than having the perfect desk ensemble. But, in reality, you probably spend more time in your work space than you do with your boss. When you're happy, comfortable, feel appreciated and rewarded, and work in an environment that suits your style and preferences, you can be more productive. That's good for you, your boss, and the company.

Once you identify those factors that you need in your work environment, it will help you understand some of your satisfaction and dissatisfaction with past workplaces. It will also help you focus on what you need to find in the future. Once you know your most important work environment factors, you can go into interviews armed with questions whose answers will help you decide if the job and company are a good fit for you. No one is advising you to accept a job just because it has great benefits, you get to wear jeans on Fridays, and it includes a paid sabbatical, but if you're on the fence about an offer, such details can be the sweet icing on the career cake.

Where Your Work Space Is

Location and how it relates to your career is dealt with in more depth in Chapter 7. Here you'll want to think about the importance of such things as whether there are parks or walking paths nearby, the workplace is in a safe neighborhood, there is adequate public transportation between your home and work, or there are nearby places to eat and shop. Some of these factors relate to your values (Chapter 2), such as access to fitness facilities, or to your work/life balance (Chapter 8), such as the amount of time your job requires you to work overtime. Of course, there are many other factors that are more important when considering your career. But just as a blister on your heel can ruin a nice walk in the loveliest of nature preserves, your dissatisfaction with seemingly minor details in your otherwise suitable work environment can accumulate to dampen your enthusiasm and eventually affect your attitude.

What Your Work Space Looks Like

Many people aspire to that quintessential corner office, the one with the windows and the spectacular view. To them, such an office signals achievement and status, regardless of the furnishings.

Some people relish working in a large, communal space where collaboration is instinctive, pet dogs roam freely, and the surroundings spark creativity and brainstorming.

Other people need to work unconstrained by the limitations of walls or furniture. Thanks to cell phones and wireless electronics, jobs that once had to be performed at a desk in an office can be done just as easily in a coffee shop or on a beach.

Whether your milieu is an old refurbished factory building or a glass-walled skyscraper, filled with music or as quiet and stark as a monastery, you will be happiest if your surroundings help you do your best work.

Silence Is Golden—or Is It?

Large numbers of technical, creative, factory, and even management workers listen to music during some portion of their workday. But there are few things less conducive to optimal work than having to listen to someone else's music that you dislike. Many workplaces still have piped-in tunes bland enough to offend no one, or inspire anyone, for that matter. Today you're more likely to find individual MP3 players in each cubicle because there are tens of millions of them in use.

The people who use MP3 players say they blot out background noise and help them stay energized. They may be on to something. Advanced Brain Technologies found that listening to some types of classical music actually makes people more productive, attentive, and on task (*www.advancedbrain.com*). But other people find music at work distracting and unprofessional. Music played through speakers can annoy those who don't share your tastes, and someone listening through headphones runs the risk of looking like a slacker. MP3s are banned completely as safety risks in workplaces where failing to hear a warning signal or another person can be dangerous. And since the devices could potentially be used to download information from office computers, they can be perceived as security risks, too.

A few companies have taken an innovative approach to the MP3 debate, using downloadable audio programs instead of meetings for training or using audio or video podcasts to keep employees updated.

The freedom to play music and podcasts may not be a deal breaker when it comes to accepting a good job, but it's something to find out about when you're researching a potential career or employer.

Body-Friendly Work Spaces

Someone once called Leonardo da Vinci the "Father of Ergonomics." If that's true, the design of furnishings and equipment to reduce human discomfort or fatigue has been around a long time, which makes it all the more surprising that it hasn't progressed further by now.

Fifty years ago, anyone with a desk job probably had a phone and perhaps a typewriter. If an uncomfortable chair gave you a sore back, or if typing reams of memos cramped your hands, or if cradling the phone all day made your neck sore—they were necessary evils associated with doing your job. Repetitive-use injuries, eyestrain, backaches, and stress just seemed like part of the package called "work," but they sometimes felt more like physical punishment.

It may be counterintuitive, but some of the twenty-first century innovative technologies that make so much work easier and faster can be even worse for the body. In 2003, according to the U.S. Census Bureau, 56.1 percent of adults in the United States used computers at work. Compare that to just 25 percent in 1984. Multitasking computers have become so useful that workers have even fewer reasons to leave their desks at all. A memo that once would have been walked up to the fifth floor is now e-mailed with a keystroke. Meetings with clients in another country can be conducted via videoconferencing. Sitting still for long periods of time causes muscle fatigue that can lead to injury. Staring at a glowing monitor for hours at a stretch provokes eyestrain and headaches. Improperly positioned chairs, desks, and keyboards encourage poor posture, neck strain, and aching backs. It goes without saying that people perform their jobs better and enjoy their work more when they're comfortable and free of pain. It helps if your work environment doesn't feel like some sort of medieval torture chamber.

Studies show that an ergonomic office environment can result in fewer sick days, fewer hours of muscle fatigue, and a greatly reduced chance of chronic disability. One furniture manufacturer asserts that in a yearlong study, people who used their chairs and received ergonomics training increased their productivity by 17.8 percent (*www.steelcase.com*). When you're researching that perfect career, try to ascertain an employer's responsiveness to ergonomic accommodations to make your workday more comfortable. Here are a few to remember:

- Adjust knee and hip angles for comfort.
- Support wrists on a padded surface, parallel to the floor.
- Use an adjustable chair with lumbar support.
- Slope the seat slightly downward to improve circulation in lower legs and feet.
- Wear a headset if you combine telephoning with hand work, such as keyboarding.
- Make sure the top line of text on your monitor is slightly below eye height.
- Eliminate glare on your computer screen.
- Look away from the screen periodically to reduce eyestrain.

Remember that even a few adjustments can help make the difference between stress and success at work. Watch out for the unintended consequences of using your laptop. In 2003, the U.S. Bureau of Labor Statistics reported that 9,200 nongovernment workers missed one day or more of work because of keyboarding-related injuries. That number is bound to go higher as more and more people work full-time on nonergonomic laptops instead of desktops. It pays to take precautions early by using peripherals, such as separate keyboards and positioning the monitor at the proper height.

How Flexible Do You Want to Be?

Some people can't work without order and systematic procedures. For them, going into a central office and knowing the workday begins at nine and ends at five gives them the structure they need. For others, "live and let live" is the motto. As long as deadlines are met and the work is good, it doesn't matter where or when it gets done. Many people are somewhere in between, perhaps working part-time, nights only, or alternating their workdays between the office and one day or two per week working from home.

The work environment is definitely changing, and the work schedule is one of the most obvious signs of that change. Many times you won't have the option of deciding your hours (for example, if you're a night security guard), but more and more workers—and employers, too—are coming to realize that a certain amount of flexibility can make for happier employees.

There are some very real benefits—to employers and workers alike—for offering and taking advantage of flexible working arrangements such as job sharing, flextime, compressed hours, or telecommuting for those positions that don't require a constant on-site presence. It's a growing trend, too. According to a 2005 benefits survey by the Society for Human Resource Management, 19 percent of companies allow some sort of job sharing, 33 percent offer a compressed workweek, 56 percent offer flextime, and 37 percent allow telecommuting. In 2005, the Dieringer Research Group found that out of 135.4 million U.S. workers, 45.1 million worked at home, as well as in other locations, such as trains, planes, parks, and in their cars (*www.workingfromanywhere.org*). Compare that to 4 million teleworkers in 1995. One report in 2000 estimated that the number of telecommuting workers in the United States would reach 100 million by 2010.

Benefits for Employees

- Enjoy better work/life balance
- Have more control over time off
- Miss fewer workdays by being able to schedule work around personal and family obligations
- Save commute time (one estimate equates a daily forty-minute commute to eight working weeks per year) and expense
- Reduce stress

- Increase productivity
- Improve morale

Benefits for Employers

- Attract and retain top talent (33 percent of the CFOs responding to a compensation survey by Robert Half International said that offering telecommuting and/or flexible work schedules was the best way to attract top talent)
- Lower administrative, real estate, and equipment costs
- Increase productivity (studies have shown productivity increases of from 15 to 38 percent)
- Make more efficient use of facilities (such as having three eight-hour shifts each day share the same work space)
- Extend customer service
- Save much of the cost of absenteeism and overtime (some say as much as $800 per worker per year)

Telecommuting

For the first time in the history of employment, the work people do is being separated from where the work gets done. Flexible working arrangements can replace some of the time spent in a central office with the option of working at home or in a local coffee shop, for that matter. Telecommuting was first tried out as a concept back in the 1970s. The array of technology available today turns just about every location into a potential work space. Equip yourself with a laptop, cell phone, wireless Internet connection, and work that doesn't have to be performed in one spot or face-to-face, and you have the makings of a telecommuter. The good news is that work can be performed anywhere. The bad news is that the work can be performed anywhere. Such freedom can turn your forty-hour-per-week job into a 24/7 grind.

In spring 2006, the Telework Coalition (*www.telcoa.org*) completed a benchmarking study of both public- and private-sector employers with large telework programs. The study focused on how these organizations addressed obstacles and overcame objections to make their programs successful. Some of the unexpected consequences of the programs included lower turnover, fewer layoffs, the ability of employees to move to other parts of the country, and the ability of the company to maintain business continuity in spite of natural or manmade disasters, such as 9/11.

Do You Like to Share?

It's possible to share office space as an employee in a large organization, as a small company just starting out, or as a solo freelancer who doesn't need a lot of space to work. The options are multiplying as the workforce becomes more mobile and flexible.

Sharing Jobs

Some jobs are too vast and complex for one person. Sometimes a person wants to work at a full-time job but doesn't want to work full time. In that case, dividing the work between two or more people makes sense. Not every occupation lends itself to this sort of split personality—less than 1 percent of the workforce has this arrangement—but if you think it could work for you, it doesn't hurt to ask. There are even online resources that sell templates for writing proposals to your boss for job sharing, telecommuting, and other flexibility options. Make sure you emphasize how the arrangement would increase productivity and benefit the company and/or the customers.

Sharing Work Spaces

Would you enjoy a shared-space work environment? Some small businesses rent space in a shared office or business center, where some of the services, such as cleaning, reception, and security, are provided. The small business gains access to meeting rooms, parking, and kitchens, without spending as much on rent. Working in a shared space with other complementary businesses improves the options for networking and referrals. There's the added advantage of increasing your social contact during the day. Studies over the past decade have shown a trend toward using more of such shared office arrangements and away from the more traditional and inflexible situations, particularly in times of economic uncertainty.

Even some large corporations use the office-sharing plan at their headquarters. AT&T and Ernst & Young use a scheme called "hoteling," where mobile workers reserve desks at the company's regular offices. Some workers stay in the same place for months, while others end up in a different place every day in office spaces that range from a small desk with a phone and a laptop port to a room the size of a phone booth with walls and a door. Sun Microsystems in Menlo Park, California, saves money by reducing the amount of space needed for each worker as they float among shared work areas.

Innovative Work Spaces

Any size company can think outside the box. *Architectural Review* detailed what it called "the office of the future" in 2003, a new complex for Norwegian telecom company Telenor. The building features an open plan in which the 6,000 workers use workstations as needed, alone, or in ever-shifting combinations. Each of the largely autonomous, thirty-person work pods has its own service and meeting areas and can be reconfigured by a crew in a short time to create separate workstations or group work spaces. No one works a full day more than a few yards from natural light. The results include lower operating costs and increased productivity.

Drop-In Centers

In 1998, Sun Microsystems opened the first of its drop-in office centers to address a critical need. Many of its engineers were tired of wasting so much time driving from all parts of the San Francisco Bay Area to the company's headquarters in Menlo Park, California, but they didn't want to work amid the distractions at home. Today there are several centers scattered throughout the Bay Area, as well as near Sun's operations in Colorado and Massachusetts. As of 2002, one-third of Sun's workers used the satellite offices, which are outfitted with computers, high-speed network connection, ergonomic furniture, and office support equipment. "Smart card" technology lets the computer recognize each worker and bring up his or her work when the person logs in. Reservations aren't permitted at the centers, which are open 24/7. Since the program's inception, Sun estimates it has saved over $300 million in IT, support, and real estate, while improving employee job satisfaction. Other companies, such as Morgan Stanley, Intel, and Fidelity Investments, have jumped on the drop-in bandwagon, too. After 9/11, they realized that smaller satellite offices have the ability to keep operating if something happens to suspend work in the main office (*www.sun.com*).

Freelancing

According to the International Telework Association and Council, the number of employed Americans working from home during business hours increased by nearly 40 percent between 2001 and 2004. Unless you've lived it, you might think the life of the freelancer is all footloose and fancy free. If anything, it can be more difficult and demanding than a regular nine-to-five job. Often it requires more organizational skill, diplomacy, and adaptability than working for one employer, not to mention the ability to weather economic uncertainty. Consider the distractions that lurk in your own home: checking the refrigerator, talking to the cat, or dusting the living room. While the refrigerator may seem less annoying than that whistling coworker, it has a Siren-like way of calling to you when a deadline looms. Even folding laundry can take on a certain new appeal on particularly unfocused days.

That's not to say you aren't suited for the freelancing life. Enterprising people are coming up with all kinds of ways to accommodate independent workers. In Santa Monica, California, one business caters to freelance writers and offers its paying members upscale surroundings, feng shui décor, power outlets, ambient wireless Internet, a library, nearby restaurants, and 24/7 access. It also posts a sign listing all the books, movies, television shows, and other works that have been written in its cozy confines.

Is the freelancing life for you? You'll find out more about your entrepreneurial abilities in Chapter 9.

The Right Perks Can Perk Up Your Career

As surprising as it might seem, salary isn't the most important factor to many people when they're searching for their ideal careers. As noted previously, even flexible work schedules can rank higher than pay, but sometimes it's the little things—the perks—that can make the difference between a so-so working environment and a stellar one. A 2005 survey by the Employment Policy Foundation found out that employees place almost as much emphasis on a benefits package as on salary when they're considering a job change. When highly qualified workers are in short supply, employers have to look for new and sometimes innovative ways to attract and retain talented people. They have come up with some interesting proposals. Some of them are inexpensive, all things considered, but some of them are not. Employers look upon these amenities as an investment and feel they pay off in the long run in happier, more productive workers who are more likely to stay. That's something that money can't always buy.

What Perks Up Your Interest?

In this age of rising health care costs, there's no question that a good health plan is a great workplace benefit. But employers admit they won't be absorbing all of the rising costs projected over the next few years. While workers pick up more of the medical tab, employers are finding other ways to improve the working environment for employees. Ample time off each year, stock options, life insurance, disability, and pension plans are fairly standard. Maternity, paternity, and family leave can help you with your work/life balance. But let's say all of your potential employers have those areas covered and offer competitive salaries. What is it going to take for you to choose one over another? Perhaps you'll be able to choose among some perks such as these from real companies. Some 14 percent of U.S. companies offered on-site conveniences in 2006. With perks like these, why would you ever go home?

- All-expense-paid trips
- Annual birthday present from employer
- Basketball, racquetball
- Child adoption expenses
- Concierge services
- Dancing classes
- Day care center
- Discounted insurance, financial planning, and other services
- Discounts on groceries, sports equipment, or cars
- Dog-friendly office
- Elder care consultation
- Giant-screen televisions for watching major sporting events after hours
- Gym memberships or on-site health club
- Housekeeping services

- Identity theft protection
- Laundry service
- Martial arts training
- Masseuse
- Meal delivery
- Mentoring program pairing new hires with veteran workers
- Oil changes and car washes
- On-site dental appointments and other health services
- On-site elementary school
- On-site haircuts and manicures
- Paid sabbaticals
- Pet care and insurance
- Prepaid legal services
- Subsidized lunches
- Themed parties
- Tuition for classes, seminars, training, or college degrees

A 2006 survey by *Money Magazine* and Salary.com confirmed the obvious: The most satisfied, least stressed workers have the best working conditions, including flexible time schedules, long vacations, and great perks. They didn't necessarily have the highest salaries, but they did often put in longer hours than their less satisfied compatriots.

Dressing for Career Success

Decades ago, most companies frowned upon individuality in one's workplace attire. Men wore dark suits, white shirts, and ties. Women wore suits, too, or appropriately subdued dresses or slacks. That's still the case in the higher echelons of some professions and occasionally is required of most businesspeople, although there are work cultures, such as in Silicon Valley, which seem to have changed all that, at least for Northern California. There you'll find workers dressed in jeans, T-shirts, and clothes once relegated to weekends or vacations. If you've never owned a suit and don't plan to, you may want to rethink that career in a high-powered New York law firm.

Decoding the Dress Codes

If a prospective employer said the dress code is "business casual," would you know exactly what that meant you could wear? Perhaps you like the idea of a job that requires a uniform. After all, people who work as nurses, police, or park rangers never have to worry about what to wear on the job. For those in careers with more relaxed dress codes, the trend seems to be toward more casual dress in the workplace. Workers definitely want it, and for employers it can prove to be a simple, inexpensive way to be flexible and improve morale. In a subtle way, it signals that promotions aren't based on social status. Khakis and polo shirts are great equalizers. In a March 2003 survey, the Business Research Lab found just 9 percent of respondents wore typical business attire to work, 50 percent wore business casual, and 41 percent wore very casual clothing (*www.busreslab.com*). A dress code can be off-putting to some potential employees, too, so a more casual approach becomes one more perk that a firm can use to hire and retain top talent.

Dress Code Dos and Don'ts

The primary considerations when it comes to suitable dress, center on propriety, neatness, and not wearing distracting or offensive clothes. Everyone seems to agree that employees with client contact should dress in business attire to maintain the air of professionalism and competence desired by all employers. Be wary of certain restrictions that could be at odds with federal antidiscrimination and disability regulations—for instance, if an employer bans ponytails or earrings for men but allows them for women, bans facial hair, or requires women to wear skirts. One dress code on a corporate Web site details its do's and don'ts right down to the removal of ear hair, the quality of toupees to be worn, and the banning of kilts, pointy-toed shoes, and "cheap" colognes and perfumes. Ask up front about the dress code for any career you're seriously considering. If you can't work unless you're wearing your bunny slippers or torn Grateful Dead T-shirt, you will know instantly which work environments to avoid.

Work Environment Test

This test doesn't cover all the variables, which are infinite, but it will give you a good idea of your general preferences. It will also point out those areas where you know you won't compromise. As before, you may want to photo-copy this test first, so you can take it again in the future. Just like interests and skills, your work environment preferences will undoubtedly change over the years. Check all the factors that are important to you. Decide which ten are of the highest priority to you and record them on your chart on page 179.

Location

❒ Close to home (within _____ minutes or _____ miles)

❒ Able to walk or bike to work

❒ Work from home

❒ Sometimes work from home

❒ Access to public transportation

❒ Access to parking

❒ Safe location

❒ Access to shops and restaurants

❒ Near parks or open space

❒ Access to a gym or health club

❒ Travel to different locations during workday

❒ U.S. travel _____ percent of time

❒ International travel _____ percent of time

❒ Other _____

Environment

❒ Cubicle

- ❏ Shared/communal work space
- ❏ Office with door
- ❏ Windows/natural light
- ❏ Bright and colorful
- ❏ Conservative and subdued
- ❏ Formal
- ❏ Casual
- ❏ Ergonomically correct
- ❏ Pets allowed
- ❏ Quiet
- ❏ Lively
- ❏ Music allowed
- ❏ Outdoors
- ❏ Mixture of indoors and outdoors
- ❏ Virtual work space
- ❏ Shared, drop-in, or "hoteling" work space
- ❏ Other _____

Schedule

- ❏ Full time
- ❏ Part time
- ❏ Set hours/schedule
- ❏ Flexible hours
- ❏ Project work
- ❏ Job share
- ❏ Telecommute

❏ Weekdays only

❏ Nights only

❏ Weekends only

❏ Specific days/months off

❏ Rotating schedule

❏ Other _____

Compensation

❏ Salary Minimum _____ Desired _____

❏ Salary plus commission

❏ Commission only

❏ Hourly rate

❏ Bonus opportunities

❏ Incentive pay

❏ Profit sharing

❏ Signing bonus

❏ Annual/quarterly bonus

❏ Stock purchase plan

❏ Stock options

❏ Other _____

Benefits

❏ Vacation (_____ weeks per year)

❏ Paid time off (set number of days to include vacation days, personal days, sick days)

❏ Unpaid vacation option

❏ Maternity/paternity/family leave

❐   Health coverage

❐   Dental coverage

❐   Vision coverage

❐   Family health coverage

❐   Tuition reimbursement

❐   401k/savings plan or 403b company contribution match

❐   Life insurance

❐   Disability insurance

❐   Professional dues

❐   Car

❐   Car expense allowance

❐   Laptop computer

❐   Cell phone

❐   Relocation fees

❐   Help with homebuying costs

❐   Health club fees

❐   Paid sabbaticals

❐   Other _____

Attire

❐   Casual

❐   Professional

❐   Personal choice

❐   Uniform

❐   Casual Friday

❐   Other _____

Type of Organization

- ❒ For profit
- ❒ Nonprofit
- ❒ Government
- ❒ Academic
- ❒ Self-employed
- ❒ Size of organization: Small _____ Medium _____ Large _____
- ❒ Business focus: Local _____ State _____ U.S. _____ International _____
- ❒ Start-up
- ❒ Established company
- ❒ Headquarters
- ❒ Branch office
- ❒ Other _____

Dena Sneider, M.A., contributed to the development of this test.

Using Your Results

Use the work environment preferences you marked here to focus your questions in informational interviews and later in job interviews. You can always ask to see the work space, especially during a second or final interview. You should be able to gauge how supportive a work environment each employer promotes by how fairly it treats its workers, if it listens to their opinions, and if it welcomes change. Study after study over the past decade has reached the same conclusion: Those workplaces that are the most employee-friendly and that display the most progressive and innovative people practices get consistently greater returns in profitability and customer satisfaction. As a potential employee with the kinds of skills and talent that a company wants, you hold a powerful trump card. If you're happy, your company will be happy. So take the time to figure out how to achieve that blissful—and profitable—balance.

Chapter 7

Location and Your Career

Location, location, location. They say it's the most important thing to remember in real estate, and it's important for your career, too. While where you work in the world may not be as critical as what work you do in the world, there is no question that location plays a large role in your career satisfaction. From cold climate to hot, mountains to seaside, foreign lands to Midwestern suburb, you'll want to carefully consider where you put your skills, talents, and abilities to work.

Location Matters

You may be thinking, "Oh, I could work anywhere." Maybe you could. If you're a computer programmer who needs to see nothing outside of a cubicle for weeks on end or a writer who needs only a laptop, then that cubicle or that laptop could probably be anyplace on earth. But your life isn't spent only at work. You have to live somewhere, perhaps with a family, certainly near friends. You likely have hobbies and activities that you want to do in your spare time that don't involve computer programming or writing. You need to shop for necessities as well as the little indulgences that make life more pleasant. You like to expand your horizons occasionally with a class or a museum visit. You enjoy a concert or movie now and then. So, if you're a computer programmer who also has a life, and your cubicle is in the middle of an isolated prairie hundreds of miles from anything, then you may be able to do your job, but you aren't going to be very happy.

Most working people can expect to change jobs several times during their lifetime, and some of those changes will entail moving someplace new. Yes, there will be considerations that will often take precedence, such as salary requirements, family obligations, or desired employer. But all other things being equal, if your employment choices are all a good match with your skills, personality, values, and interests, then the location of your work can be an important determining factor in your career path. There will be certain places that suit you, speak to you, and enable you to work more efficiently, effectively, and contentedly.

Live Where the Surroundings Please You

Many people thrive in the bustle of a big city environment. They like to take public transportation to work or walk to the local deli. For them, the accessibility of nightlife, cultural attractions, civic parks, and other amenities make the crowding, noise, anonymity, and expense all worth it.

Then there are those who would rather die than live removed from the great outdoors, who need access to mountain biking or hiking trails, lakes for fishing and boating, rocks for climbing, or slopes for skiing and boarding. There are those who would feel lost without the cocoon of small-town familiarity, where they feel safe and know every neighbor and shopkeeper for blocks. Still others revel in the kid-friendly suburbs, full of shopping malls, golf courses, and dog parks.

Don't forget climate. Any of the preceding can be located in areas where winter lasts six months or one week, where there's rain every day or not at all, or anything in between. If you love seasons, then Southern California may not be the place for you. If you love cloudy days and rain, you might want to consider the Pacific Northwest.

Depending on your situation, your requirements, and your desires, you can find a place that furthers your career and feeds your soul.

Live Where You Have Support

In past centuries in the United States (and still in many parts of the world today), extended families lived together in the same town, in the same neighborhood, or under the same roof. Elders looked after grandchildren, and siblings worked with parents. One's extended family was nearby to offer moral and financial support in the bad times and celebrate milestones, birthdays, and other occasions in the good.

Today that isn't always the case. College, jobs, or marriage can take people across the country—or the world—and far away from their families, old friends, and the places where they grew up. Unless you're adept at forging deep friendships quickly, you may not develop the social support network of family, friends, and coworkers in your new place that you had in the old. Sometimes such a lack of community can lead to loneliness. Research has shown that social isolation has real detrimental health effects, such as high blood pressure, disrupted sleep, and depression. Indeed, some researchers surmise that loneliness can be as bad for your health as a poor diet or lack of exercise.

Life-changing circumstances, such as having a child, becoming seriously ill, or natural or other disasters, such as hurricanes or 9/11, can change your perspective on where you want to live. You may want to move closer to family or friends to enjoy the benefits of a close-knit social and emotional support system. Most people want to feel safe and secure in their surroundings. In 2006, North Dakota was ranked the country's

Safest State for the ninth time by the Morgan Quitno Press. Other states on the "safe" list include Maine, Vermont, New Hampshire, and Wyoming. Out of 369 cities considered, the country's safest include Newton, Massachusetts; Clarkstown, New York; and Mission Viejo, California. The rankings are based on FBI data for murder, burglary, motor vehicle theft, and other factors.

Support can include other things besides family, too. Some people prefer to be near those who share their heritage or speak their native language, even if they aren't related. Many people whose religious beliefs form an integral part of who they are want to reside in a community that shares their faith. Other forms of support include excellent health care facilities, educational opportunities if you decide to advance or change careers, affordable child care, and good public transportation systems.

Depending on your circumstances, any combination of these factors can dramatically affect your choice of location.

Live in an Area You Can Afford

Every year, several different organizations list the world's most expensive cities in which to live. In this country, they usually include New York, Boston, Washington, D.C., Los Angeles, and San Francisco. Overseas, you'll pay a lot to live in Tokyo, London, Moscow, Seoul, Geneva, Milan, or Paris. When deciding on a career opportunity and where you want to live, it's good to know up front if you'd need to spend over $4,500 per month for a two-bedroom unfurnished apartment in Tokyo or need an annual salary of $65,000 to cover the basic needs of a family of four in Boston.

Recent U.S. Census data (May 2006) tracks the growing exodus from high-priced city centers and suburbs into smaller "micropolitan" towns with populations between 10,000 and 49,000 and even farther out into areas that until now were forests or farms. New York, San Francisco/Oakland, Chicago, and Los Angeles averaged net outflows of more than 60,000 people per year. Some experts see this pattern as part of the country's continuing transition from a manufacturing to a service-oriented economy. While the out-migration has a lot to do with finding affordable housing, some experts fear that it could overwhelm these more sparsely populated areas that lack the infrastructure to accommodate thousands of new residents.

Americans are a highly mobile society; everybody knows that, right? Yes, but not in the way you might think. Back in the eighteenth and nineteenth centuries, wagonloads of pioneers did strike out to lay claim to the wide-open spaces beyond the Appalachian Mountains. In later decades, people flooded from farm to city to suburb. This mobility left such a lasting impression that we think it continues to this day. The most recent U.S. Census data say otherwise. In 2003, only 14 percent of this country's residents moved, the lowest rate since this information has been tracked starting in 1948.

There are many reasons cited for this change. More people are willing to commute longer distances to work (see Chapter 8 for more about commuting); there are more dual-income households, which are less portable than the one-income, one-stay-at-home parent model; more people own rather than rent their living quarters; and there are more Baby Boomers and others who stay put because of elder care responsibilities.

Live Where It's Livable

"Livability" means different things to different people. You may seek a community by prioritizing one characteristic, such as where people are considered well educated and more literate, such as those in Seattle, Minneapolis, Washington, D.C., or Boston. The definition of livability has also changed over the years. Some small communities were once too isolated to be considered desirable, until the Internet came along.

Today, organizations such as Partners for Livable Communities (PLC) (*www.mostlivable.org*) assess many factors to track the livability of communities, cities, and states. It isn't all about work. As St. Paul, Minnesota, Mayor Randy Kelly said in a 2004 *USA Today* interview, "People are hungering to live in communities that are safe, clean, and affordable and have a sense of place and the kinds of amenities that enrich their lives." PLC identifies several hallmarks of livable communities—"Creative Places"—which notably include attitudes, not physical characteristics such as buildings or parks. These hallmarks include:

- Stimulates physical, mental, and spiritual potential of individuals
- Fosters good schools, jobs, housing, public transportation, clean air, and safety
- Encourages a harmonious relationship between humans and nature
- Helps conserve energy and natural resources
- Brings quality to the physical, social, economic, and cultural environment
- Encourages choices and opportunities
- Takes advantage of its unique features
- Understands a community's roots
- Develops a participatory attitude

Remember that livability to you may not be the same as livability to someone else. The following test will help you pinpoint your most desired characteristics in a location, which will help you refine your career trajectory.

Location Test

Check all of the location requirements that are important to you or that interest you now. If you select "Other," jot down your ideas about what that "other" might be in the space provided. Also write notes if you have more specific ideas than are represented by these broad categories. For example, if you know you want to work in New Hampshire, write that next to "Northeast."

United States
- ❒ Northeast
- ❒ Mid-Atlantic
- ❒ Southeast
- ❒ Midwest
- ❒ Southwest
- ❒ Rocky Mountains
- ❒ West Coast
- ❒ Northwest

❏ Other _____

International
❏ Africa
❏ Asia
❏ Australia/New Zealand
❏ Canada
❏ Europe
❏ Middle East
❏ South America
❏ Other _____

Setting
❏ Urban
❏ Suburban
❏ Small town
❏ Rural
❏ Other _____

Climate
❏ Varied
❏ Mostly warm
❏ Mostly cool

Access to Resources
❏ Family/significant others
❏ Friends
❏ Similar ethnic group
❏ Multicultural community
❏ Public transportation
❏ Major airport
❏ Health care
❏ Education
❏ Cultural amenities
❏ Community
❏ Religious/spiritual

❑ Nature
❑ Shopping
❑ Sports and recreation
❑ Other _____

Now look back over your choices and circle your top eight requirements. Write these items in the following spaces and in your chart on page 179.

My Top Eight Location Requirements

1. _____
2. _____
3. _____
4. _____
5. _____
6. _____
7. _____
8. _____

Terry Karp, M.A., contributed to the development of this test.

Using Your Results

Now that you've identified the where, investigate the how. Many large bookstores or well-stocked newsstands have newspapers from other cities and countries. Read a few issues, or if you're really serious, subscribe. You'll learn about local news, plus the papers will include want ads with job openings, real estate information, and much more. Follow regional hiring trends in the locations you're considering. The U.S. Bureau of Labor Statistics (*www.bls.gov*) describes occupations in demand and where hiring is strongest, as well as salary information. Online resources include Morgan Quitno Press (*www.morganquitno.com*), which rates cities and states by a variety of factors, such as safety and health. Also review corporate literature and Web sites in your top locations.

Use Your Contacts

Experts will tell you that most job openings aren't formally advertised, and that's why it's crucial to network. That same network of colleagues, friends, neighbors, mentors, and family can help you scope out a new location, too. If you belong to a church or national organization (Lions Club, Girl Scouts) or professional organizations (American Association of University Women, American Association of Museums), you can put those contacts to use in researching your new location. At the very least, such organizations give you a ready-made base of acquaintances. Beyond that, those associates all have resources, contacts, and information to share about their particular location.

Use Free Government Resources

There are many resources that will help you learn all you can about the region or community to which you are thinking about moving. Statistics on employment, housing, income, and much more—information that used to be available only by phone or mail—are now available on the Internet. Contact the local chamber of commerce (*www.chamberofcommerce.com*) or U.S. Bureau of Labor Statistics (*www.bls.gov*).

Use Relocation Web Sites

Many of them have long quizzes that will provide you with a list of communities to suit your answers. There you'll find commentaries on the livability of various places around the world, as well as information about projects designed to make cities and small towns more people-friendly. Some, such as *www.bestplaces.net*, offer information about school districts, crime rates, cost of living, and housing, as well as candid opinions of different cities posted by people who live or have lived there. Some, such as *www.escapeartist .com/expatriate/resources.htm*, focus on what you need to know to live overseas.

Take a Vacation

If the location you're thinking about moving to is far away, exotic, and/or quite different from your current circumstances, consider going there for a visit before packing up and moving there.

Look Around

If you're visiting the new location for a job interview, schedule some other time to check out schools, neighborhoods, and cultural amenities. Sometimes just walking around a place can give you more information than any number of brochures or Web sites.

Take a Temporary Job

To make really sure that a permanent move will be right for you, you can test the waters by taking a temporary house-sitting or caretaking position and get to know the locals (*www.caretaker.org*).

Remember, when you're trying to get the full picture of your own criteria for career satisfaction, physical location plays an important role.

Chapter 8

Work/Life Balance and Your Career

You need only look around your neighborhood and workplace to see how stressful your life has become. On any given day you probably have too much to do and too many decisions to make. Job security is no longer a given. You worry about the safety of your loved ones at a time when terrorism, natural disasters, and societal problems fill the news. It is critical for your career satisfaction that you strike the right balance between work and the obligations, wants, and needs that fill your personal life.

8

A Life Out of Balance

If you believe your life is in perfect balance and that harmony reigns supreme at home and at work, then by all means, skip to Chapter 9. The odds are good, however, that there are times when your job swallows up your home life with early mornings, late evenings, long commutes, bulging briefcases of paperwork to be done after hours, and even weekend stints in the office to finish a report before Monday. Americans are obsessed by—some would say defined by—their work. Who hasn't attended a party and been asked, "What do you do?" In many other countries, work provides the means to enjoy the rest of one's life. In the United States, we are conditioned from an early age to focus on what we want to be when we grow up and then set about working toward that goal, not just achieving it but excelling at it. Success, recognition, and lots of money are great, but if they come at the expense of your family, friendships, health, and even sanity, are they truly worth it?

9 to 5 Is Now 24/7

As globalization revs into high gear, it seems there is more work to do in a shorter amount of time than ever before. Budget cuts, downsizing, layoffs, and early retirement packages have left fewer workers to do the same work, or more, while employers want more work done for less cost. It's not unusual at some companies for one or two people to handle the work that five used to do. Pagers, e-mail, cell phones, and other technologies can make jobs immeasurably more efficient, but they also mean that you can never truly be out of reach of the office or its demands. There's always the danger of being perceived as not working hard enough if you don't respond immediately to every message you get.

Probing the Problem

There is no shortage of surveys, studies, commissions, and task forces striving to draw attention to the fact that U.S. workers are increasingly stressed out and overworked. Even the Senate took note in 2003, when it passed a bipartisan resolution declaring October as National Work and Family Month, stating that, "reducing the conflict between work and family life should be a national priority." The appendices at the back of this book can direct you to some of the research organizations and the studies they conduct. Some of their findings in recent years include these illuminating facts.

- One in three employees claims to be chronically overworked.
- Men work on average forty-nine paid and unpaid hours per week, while women average forty-three and one-half hours.
- Half of those asked in one survey said they felt overwhelmed by their workload the previous month.
- Only 36 percent of workers feel truly secure in their jobs.
- Many workers feel they would be penalized if they took advantage of the work/life options their employers offer.
- Over one-third of workers have no plans to take all of the vacation time they are due.

Here's a depressing thought: In 2005, a researcher at McKinsey & Company noted, "We have created jobs that are literally impossible." Even with twice as much time available, managers agree that they would still not get everything done. The problem can be particularly severe for freelancers and entrepreneurs. That kind of work can be feast-or-famine, and so to forestall the famine, the self-employed say "yes" to every project, filling every moment with work because next week there may be none.

Not Your Grandpa's Workplace

Remember the good old days of guaranteed lifetime employment? Didn't think so. Today, the average worker changes jobs five to seven times during a career. Seniority no longer equals job security.

Decades ago, former General Electric CEO Jack Welch was a young workaholic slaving away in the office on Saturdays. As he wrote in *Winning,* "I thought these weekend hours were a blast. The idea just didn't dawn on me that anyone would want to be anywhere but at work." Well, they did, whether they said so or not. Today's workers are less shy about saying so.

The Baby Boom generation shook things up, shattering glass ceilings and fighting for maternity leave, civil rights, equal opportunity, and equal rights while inventing the personal computer, the Pill, the power suit, and no-fault divorce along the way.

Once women had muscled their way into the boardroom, they worked whatever punishing hours they had to in order to stay there, even if it meant postponing marriage, babies, or a personal life.

Today's younger workers are taking it to a whole new level. These are the innovators who have embraced high-tech gadgets and turned them into a lifestyle. With their BlackBerries, cell phones, laptops, Palm Pilots, and pagers, they can take their work everywhere and anywhere. In a sense, they've created their own monster. In survey after survey, the younger generation of workers ranks time off as a top priority. In one 2004 study by the Society for Human Resource Management, work/life balance was their number two concern, right after compensation.

Family Matters

Increasing research focuses on today's working families, how they're changing, and how they're juggling the relationship between home and work. Eighty-five percent of U.S. workers live with family members, which increases the day-to-day responsibilities away from their workplace. Research by the Alfred P. Sloan Center on Parents, Children, and Work has shown that the conflict between job and family causes both to suffer. Highly stressed workers are more likely to bring work home and feel angry and exhausted when they are home.

Your parents or grandparents may recall the days when dad brought home the bacon and mom stayed home to care for the 2.5 children. Less than 20 percent of today's workforce has such a "traditional" family structure. Most mothers are now working outside the home: 80 percent of working women are mothers. They're feeling the crunch. By a margin of almost two to one, young working mothers value flexibility over advancement at work. As the schedules of many middle school students grow to resemble those of busy CEOs, the shuttling and chaperoning duties fall to already overburdened parents. Add to that the fact that one quarter of U.S. workers provide care for an elder, and you have the ingredients for worker burnout.

Men Want a Life, Too

Men may be from Mars and women from Venus, but apparently they are much more alike in their desire for work/life balance than was previously assumed. Research shows that fathers are doing more child care than they used to. A 2005 survey of Fortune 500 male senior executives found that the younger the executive, the more likely it was that he cared about having more balance between his work and personal life. Half of them wondered if the sacrifices they've made for their careers are worth it, and over half would be willing to sacrifice income for more time away from work. Most of those surveyed thought it was possible to restructure jobs so they could have more time for things outside work and still achieve their professional goals. But here's the rub—most of them felt that bringing up these issues to the boss would hurt their careers.

They are going to have to find ways to do it. Psychologists acknowledge that your happiness is more likely to come from your loved ones than from work. The strength you derive from them will fuel your job success. In a *Fortune Magazine* profile, CEO David Neeleman remembers being caught up in what he termed the "money, power, and glory" when JetBlue went public in 2001. The head of his church brought him back to earth by reminding him that, "It's all about your family, your relationships. You've got to balance that with your work." From that moment on, Neeleman made sure that most evenings and weekends were designated family time. The decision had a positive effect on his family—and his business. With life harmonious at home, "you can be a lot more focused at work," he says.

Going to Extremes

The next time you find yourself grumbling about your twenty-minute drive to work, consider this: The winner of a 2006 nationwide contest to find the longest commute was a Californian who drives 357 miles to work and back every day—that's seven hours behind the wheel every day. His commute may be unusual, but his case is only one in a growing trend. The average commute in this country is fifty minutes. Those so-called "extreme commuters" spend a minimum of three hours traveling to and from work. According to the U.S. Census Bureau, the ranks of extreme commuters have jumped 95 percent since 1990.

One reason for the long commutes is that affordable housing and high salaries aren't always found in the same place. In what's termed the "commuting paradox," commuters accept the burden of a long drive in exchange for something of value: a better school district, bigger house, or higher salary. In reality, the tradeoff doesn't seem to be worth it. Studies show that, on average, commuters are much less satisfied with their lives than noncommuters are. Economists at the University of Zurich's Institute for Empirical Research in Economics say that people usually overestimate the value of the things they'll gain by commuting and underestimate the value of what they're giving up—their social life, family time, health, or hobbies.

Even if you don't have a long commute, you are still spending more and more time in your car. The Texas Transportation Institute says that the average annual traffic delay per rush-hour traveler has increased from sixteen hours in 1982 to forty-seven hours in 2003. Nationwide, that's 3.7 billion hours wasted in traffic delays and billions of wasted gallons of gas, increased congestion, and worsening pollution.

But just to prove that there is no one-size-fits-all where work/life balance is concerned, remember that California commuter? His job satisfaction, commute, and lifestyle suit him just fine.

Who Needs Balance?

Everyone needs balance. Without balance in our lives and workplaces, we miss much of the joy, beauty, and grandeur of life. If most of your days and nights are focused on doing, striving, and achieving, and your so-called free time is spent in fiercely competitive play or struggling for perfection in yourself or your relationships, you may have very little time and energy left to appreciate your accomplishments or leave any room for spontaneity, serendipity, or simply being, which is as crucial to human life as air, water, and laughter.

Unfortunately, it may take awhile for most businesses to catch on. A 2003 article in the *Harvard Business Review* defines people who highly value work/life balance as "B players," or second-tier workers. Declaring an interest in a humanely scaled job could, in some organizations, spell the demise of your career. Victorian writer John Ruskin listed three things that people need in order to be happy in their work. Besides being fit for it and deriving a sense of success from it, he said you "must not do too much of it." It's up to you to determine what "too much" of it is. As Xerox CEO Anne Mulcahy once said, "Businesses need to be 24/7. Individuals don't."

Work/Life Balance Test

The purpose of this test is to give you the opportunity to think about and evaluate the balance between your work life and your personal life. Use the following scale to indicate how accurately each statement describes your feelings or beliefs.

0	Not applicable
1	Usually true
2	Sometimes true
3	Almost never true

	I like my job more often than not.
	My supervisor is supportive of my efforts to lead a balanced life.
	I am generally able to choose when I can take my vacation.
	My organization supports the importance of family, leisure time, and physical health.
	I have control over my working and nonworking lives.
	I do not have difficulty relaxing at home.
	I get enough sleep.
	I have time for quiet and introspection.
	I do not have to work on my normal days off.
	I have a good circle of friends.
	On weekends I am able to enjoy the things I do.
	The quality of my work is good.

	I am satisfied with the amount of time I am able to spend with friends and family.
	The amount of travel required for my job is compatible with my personal life.
	I do not have to take work home with me in the evenings.
	I find time for my hobbies and volunteer work.
	I exercise regularly.
	I can put my job out of my mind when I am home.
	I maintain a healthy and balanced diet.
	I keep informed about developments in my organization.
	I am liked by my coworkers.
	I am able to develop my skills and abilities in this job.
	My personal life does not interfere with my job.
	I am able to fulfill my spiritual needs.
	My job allows me to be the kind of spouse/partner/parent I want to be.
	I find time to handle urgent personal situations.
	My work is personally fulfilling.
	My personal life does not make me tired at work.
	My organization supports its employees in being involved in the community.
	I do not abuse drugs, alcohol, or food.
	I have at least one person with whom I can share my thoughts and feelings.
	I feel good about myself.
	= My Work/Life Balance Score

Scoring Your Test

If you scored 32 or less: You are doing a good job of finding balance between your work and personal life.

If your score was 33 to 64: You probably need to work on certain areas to get more balance.

If your score was 65 or more: You need to seriously address the issues contributing to imbalance between your work and personal life.

Regardless of your score, but particularly if you scored over 33, circle one to three statements that represent areas that you feel could stand some improvement. Recast these as goal statements. For example, if you answered "almost never true" to the statement "I exercise regularly," rewrite it as "I want to take positive steps to incorporate regular exercise into my week." Write these statements in your chart on page 179.

Mark Guterman, M.A., contributed to the development of this test.

Using Your Results

Your test score may have opened your eyes to some areas of your life that are out of balance. More probably, it reconfirmed what you already knew. It should, at the very least, give you one or two areas for improvement. Finding work/life balance involves tradeoffs and setbacks. But the potential rewards are so great that you owe it to yourself to try.

Balance Is Good for Your Health

With balance in your personal life and work, you can be more creative, productive, healthy, and satisfied. Studies have shown that working parents who spend time with their family report feeling happier and more relaxed, as well as feeling more engaged when they're at work.

When your work and personal life are out of balance, you are apt to be forced to use much of your energy—consciously or otherwise—in an effort to regain balance. That sense of imbalance can negatively impact your level of satisfaction, sense of well-being, mental health, physical health, and job performance. Research has found that stressed-out employees are more depressed and make more mistakes. High stress has been proven to contribute to heart disease, high blood pressure, eczema, migraines, sleep disorders, increased anger levels, and fatigue. Plus One Fitness in New York found that workers who make the time to exercise 100 days per year or more use 30 percent fewer sick days than those who exercise less.

Excessive commuting is associated with raised blood pressure, musculoskeletal disorders, increased hostility, lateness, absenteeism, and adverse effects on cognitive performance. Robert D. Putnam, the author of *Bowling Alone: The Collapse and Revival of American Community*, (Simon and Schuster) says that for every ten minutes of commuting time, one's social connections get cut by 10 percent. Let's see. That means a commute of two hours would equate to no social life whatsoever.

Balance Is Good for Business

The U.S. workplace is shifting away from the old military model of top-down chain of command to more of a partnership between boss and staff. Organizations may come to resemble jigsaw puzzles instead of pyramids as they learn to piece together and accommodate a mélange of work arrangements. This collaborative atmosphere has great potential for helping workers find their work/life balance.

When businesses fail to recognize their employees' need for work/life balance, it can lead to poor performance, increased absenteeism, sick leave, higher turnover, and higher costs. Companies have a vested interest in keeping valuable employees. The average cost of losing an employee is one and one-half times the employee's annual salary, when you take into account lost productivity while the position is open and the cost of recruiting, training, and hiring a replacement. The consensus among those who study these issues is that employees who have options are more satisfied and willing to put in extra effort. When employees are happy, business thrives. Martin Baily, chair of the Council of Economic Advisors during the Clinton Administration, noted that, "There is probably not a productivity penalty to shortening hours in the U.S., and there may even be a benefit." He was right. A 2003 study by the nonprofit Families and Work Institute found that executives who worked five fewer hours per week were more productive than others who worked longer hours.

Joe Robinson, author of *Work to Live* (Perigee Trade) and founder of a group by the same name, advocates passing a law for a three-week paid minimum leave in this country and making Election Day a holiday. While other countries add weeks to their vacation policies, Americans ratchet up the overtime.

Not every option is going to be right for every business, but there are probably some that will work in your situation. If flexibility leads to happier workers who are more committed to their jobs, how could that be bad for business?

Take Action

There are many options for bringing more equilibrium to your situation. Some will work for you; others will not. Even a decision that's right for you now may not work six months from now. Studies show that most employees don't even take advantage of the flexibility benefits their employers do offer. Don't assume the answer is "no" if you don't even bother to ask. Investigate and initiate. All you have to gain is a life.

Customize Your Career

This is a growing trend that combines life planning and job flexibility, allowing you to examine and prioritize career/life tradeoffs. Take a tip from business schools, including Wharton, Harvard, and Stanford, all of which offer courses on integrating work and home life: Inventory the most important things in your work and family life; solicit support from employer and family; and try solutions until you find the best way to accomplish your goals.

Take Advantage of Employer Programs or Benefits

While surveys have found that some organizations offer only the bare minimum, nearly 60 percent of companies offer flextime programs, and many offer company-sponsored education, flexible career paths, maternity and paternity leave, or the opportunity to work from home.

Redefine Success

The tests in this book can help you. Then let your employer know what you need. Most employers will appreciate your candor and initiative. Xerox CEO Anne Mulcahy encourages her best employees to come forward with ideas on how to make things work. "Innovative job design is the way to keep great people," she says.

Work Smarter, Not Longer

A 2003 study by Marakon Associates and the Economist Intelligence Unit found that as much as 80 percent of top management time is taken up by issues that account for less than 20 percent of the company's long-term value. In 2002, the United States was less productive per hour worked than France, Belgium, Germany, Norway, and the Netherlands, where workers spent fewer hours working per week.

Find out if you can work for six months and take off one. Take on fewer clients. Work nine to four, five days per week, but longer hours at crunch times.

Share the Job

Work three days per week instead of seven, twenty to twenty-five hours instead of fifty to sixty. Many people in this arrangement find that they're better able to focus at work, since work is no longer encroaching on their home lives.

In 1997, both Gary Newman and Dana Walden were appointed president of 20th Century Fox Television—not to share one job but to both manage all aspects of a highly complex job. The arrangement has improved productivity at work and quality family time at home. The *Los Angeles Times* accomplished the same thing when the managing editor's position was split. On the surface, these solutions look expensive, but the improvement in productivity has far outweighed the cost.

Take a Sabbatical

Some companies give employees paid sabbaticals, saying it reduces turnover and retains talent otherwise lost to burnout. In 2005, the *Journal of Education for Business* published a study that found that the use of sabbaticals is growing rapidly outside academia and has positive effects on both employers and employees. The Society for Human Resource Management finds that 5 percent of corporate respondents to their annual survey offer paid sabbaticals, and another 18 percent offer unpaid ones.

Use Teamwork

Teams in some other countries and cultures function differently from those in the United States. Leslie Perlow, a Harvard Business School ethnographer, studied teams of software engineers around the world. Only in Hungary did the system allow for a life outside the office. In Hungary, any engineer with a question could go to any available colleague. The team systems in other countries led to burnout or longer hours. Interestingly, none of the teams studied thought there was any other way to do the work.

Other Ideas

Here are some more things you can do to find balance in your life. Remember, if you can't achieve or maintain balance in your current position, you might have to find a workplace that better suits your priorities. Look at lists of the best companies to work for, such as the Fortune 100 and the Working Mother lists.

- Go on a "technology fast." Turn off all machines—fax, phone, computer, television, radio, e-mail, cell phone, and pager. Whether for thirty minutes, an hour, or a day, it can be re-energizing to give all of your attention to your family or yourself.
- Negotiate a more flexible schedule. For example, no work on most weekends, a workweek of four ten-hour days, or starting work earlier so you can pick the kids up in the afternoon. Explain how the change will benefit the company.
- Negotiate your own rate of promotion. Rather than put in the bone-crushing hours necessary to move up through the ranks in three years, choose a longer period of time to accomplish the same goal.
- Sign up for a life planning course. There are many courses that integrate long-term planning for career, home, finances, and even spirituality.
- Keep your sense of humor. Surely your boss can't be as bad as that pointy-haired guy in the "Dilbert" cartoons or Dagwood Bumstead's boss, Mr. Dithers.
- Keep it all in perspective. Meg Whitman, CEO of eBay, tells the story of being in New York and watching the ticker as her company went public. She called her neurosurgeon husband in the operating room to share the news. "That's nice," he said, "But Meg, remember, it's not brain surgery."

Add Exercise to Your Day

You don't have to train for the Iron Man. One-half hour of cardio exercise three or four times per week provides health benefits. Stretches and breathing exercises can help alleviate stress. Get up a little earlier for some yoga, take the stairs instead of the elevator, take a walk at lunchtime, park your car at the far end of the lot, or join a gym (if your company has an on-site fitness facility, so much the better). If you enlist a workout buddy or spend money to take classes, you'll be less inclined to blow it off.

To Balance or Not to Balance?

There's an ongoing debate among work/life experts about the word "balance" in this context. Many argue that searching for some sort of equilibrium turns the struggle into an either/or concept. Making work and home demands equal—when one loses, the other gains—makes the goal of "balance" unachievable. They prefer the term work/life "effectiveness," where one can excel and grow at work while having access to the policies and programs that support one's personal life, too. Whether you call it "balance" or "effectiveness," all agree on its benefits and desirability.

None but the irredeemably workaholic has ever said with a straight face, "I wish I'd spent more time at the office." Don't wait until your retirement party to wonder why you didn't take that trip around the world when you were young, or rue the fact that you missed every one of your child's birthday parties, or regret that you never learned to paint or play the flugelhorn. Don't believe it when you hear you can't have it all. "All" means different things to different people. Maybe you can have it all, without having to choose between your work and your life. You just have to figure out what your "all" is and balance your life and work so that you can achieve it.

Chapter 9

Entrepreneurial Readiness and Your Career

Perhaps you feel stifled by your boss or corporate structure. Do you wonder "is this all there is" while completing yet one more task for someone else? Maybe you've promised yourself that you will start your own business the moment you find the right opportunity. Even if you don't think of yourself as the entrepreneurial type, you might already have some of the characteristics of one. As you ponder your career choices, consider that this could be the right time to become your own boss.

What Is an Entrepreneur?

An entrepreneur is someone who organizes, operates, and assumes the risk of a business venture. Add to that "in return for profits," and you have a fairly common description of the term. Some would also add "using good judgment" to that definition, particularly in situations where reliable data and previous experience don't exist, situations all too common for the entrepreneur.

Even if you can't define *entrepreneur*, you know one when you see one. Any schoolchild can rattle off the names of some famous ones: Henry Ford, Thomas Edison, Bill Gates, Martha Stewart, and Jenny Craig, to name a few. If you don't know the names of others, you surely know their enterprises: Howard Schultz of Starbucks, Jeff Bezos of Amazon, Ray Kroc of McDonald's, Chester Carlson of Xerox, and Anita Roddick of The Body Shop. Entrepreneurs are particularly esteemed in the United States because of their perceived adventurous outlook, drive, and individualism. These qualities mirror the way the country likes to see itself. After all, America was founded by entrepreneurial types who risked life and limb for the promise of untold riches on an uncharted continent. Any culture that values and rewards the self-made man or woman will encourage entrepreneurship. In 2004, Treasury Secretary John Snow acknowledged another key aspect of entrepreneurship when he said, "We've got to let people fail, and [not] make failure a lifelong stigma." He went on to recognize the value of these unique people to the economy: "We need to keep the entrepreneurs and the spirit of [entrepreneurship] strong."

Who Wants to Be an Entrepreneur?

Lots of people, apparently. In the 1980s, becoming an entrepreneur was looked upon as slightly unusual. Only a tiny percentage of graduating MBAs considered it. At that time, entrepreneurs enjoyed something of a cult status. You no doubt have heard of those renegades Steve Jobs and Steve Wozniak. By 2000, the idea of going into business for oneself had become almost de rigueur. That year, a Kauffman Center for Entrepreneurial Leadership survey found that 65 percent of fourteen- to nineteen-year-olds expressed an interest in starting their own businesses. In 2001, U.S. Bureau of Labor Statistics figures showed that about 6.5 percent of the U.S. workforce identified themselves as independent contractors. An increasing number of those self-employed entrepreneurs are women. In 2003, Secretary of Labor Elaine Chao said, "Women-owned businesses are growing at twice the rate of all U.S. firms. . . . From 1997 to 2000, women-owned businesses with $1 million or more in revenue grew 31 percent, while their male-owned counterparts grew by just 19 percent."

Who Will Become an Entrepreneur?

Remember the "Peter Principle"? Lawrence Peter maintained that workers get promoted until they reach the level of their incompetence. That might be one reason to leave an organization and strike out on your own. Daniel H. Pink, author of *Free Agent Nation,* gives another: the "Peter-Out Principle," which says that workers will rise through the ranks until they reach that level where they stop having fun. Do you prefer doing the work to managing others who do it? Then you might be a good candidate for entrepreneurship.

Any number of entrepreneurs can't be too many for some people. Peter Jones, a self-described "serial entrepreneur" and proprietor of *Dragon's Den* on the BBC, considers entrepreneurs the equivalent of rock stars and says, "I've always liked the idea of creating a nation of entrepreneurs." The United States seems to be well on its way. Perhaps you'll be one of them.

A Short History of Entrepreneurs

Before charging down that path to entrepreneurship, you might want to know a little more about the origin of the whole concept. While the word entrepreneur has been around only since the eighteenth century, people we would recognize as entrepreneurs have been around since humans first figured out that they needed to work in order to make a living. But entrepreneurs haven't always been seen in the positive terms of today, nor have they always been so admired.

Adventurer and Risk-Bearer

In 1755, Richard Cantillon wrote the first clear definition of an entrepreneur, which was translated in English as "adventurer," as an agent who buys materials or products at certain prices with the ultimate purpose of selling those products in the future. For Cantillon, the uncertainty of those future prices is what set the entrepreneur apart from other types of business-men. Adventurers actively traded and traveled, used their wits to survive, and made up the skills they needed as they went along, often quite liter-ally risking their lives along with their capital. John Jacob Astor, founder of the American Fur Company, is just one example of this early entrepreneur, as well as this country's first millionaire. Since Cantillon's book wasn't pub-lished until two decades after his death, he wasn't around to witness the response to his ideas.

Innovator, Commercializer, and Organizer

Physician and economist François Quesnay published his economic theories in 1758 and focused on the entrepreneur's ability to organize and innovate. He was something of an entrepreneur himself. Poor and orphaned at thirteen, he trained himself in medicine and economics and became a physician at the court of Louis XV.

Another famed economist, Adam Smith, maintained that people are nat-urally industrious, not entrepreneurial. With the publication of his *Inquiry into the Nature and Causes of the Wealth of Nations* in 1776, entrepreneurs lost standing; indeed, one later economist said Smith rendered the entrepre-neur invisible.

It was Jean-Baptiste Say who resuscitated entrepreneurs and empha-sized their role in an economy. After reading Smith's book, Say published his own in 1803. In it he came up with the concept (if not the exact words) of "supply creates its own demand." He deemed entrepreneurs critical to the operation of every sort of industry because they organize the "factors of production" in order to achieve the "satisfaction of human wants." He noted that entrepreneurs aren't merely managers but also forecasters, risk-takers, and project appraisers—indeed, the indispensable ones who make an economy work.

Later, in 1848, John Stuart Mill popularized "entrepreneur" in his *Princi-ples of Political Economy,* but the concept lapsed back into obscurity by the end of the nineteenth century.

Unique Individual

In 1876, Francis Walker helped resurrect the importance of the entrepreneur, writing that the "pride of directing great operations and the sense of power in moving masses of men at will . . . in no inconsiderable degree . . . make up the remuneration of the entrepreneur." He acknowledged that only a very few people were driven by these motivations.

Hero and Creative Destroyer

In the 1930s, Austrian economist Joseph Schumpeter depicted the entrepreneur as an innovative hero. His description sounds more like that of a Knight of the Round Table, someone driven by the "dream and the will to found a private kingdom," "the impulse to fight," and the "joy of creating." Schumpeter theorized that in the absence of innovation, business cycles circle in a stationary loop. The entrepreneur, by leading the way in creating new industries, disturbs this equilibrium and drives economic development. This process of rendering old industries obsolete was called "creative destruction." Think about what happened to the ticker tape, typewriter, and horse and buggy when new and better innovations came along—dreamed up and promoted by entrepreneurs.

Engager of Uncertainty and Everyman

Chicago economist Frank Knight refined Cantillon's ideas and identified an entrepreneur as one who stakes his money and career on an uncertain venture. Risk is insurable. Knight contended that profits come from uncertainty, unique events that can't be eliminated or insured against. That entrepreneur who can rely on good judgment to choose the right course of action will win the profits. Unfortunately for the entrepreneur, after enough instances of a given situation, the uncertainty becomes a knowable risk, and profits dwindle.

In the 1970s, Nobel Laureate Theodore W. Schultz found entrepreneurs everywhere. He noted that farmers and housewives deal with costs, returns, and risks; perceive, interpret, and act in response to new information; and allocate time and resources. To him, entrepreneurship was a process that occurred all around us, not solely in the business world.

Despite the best efforts of theorists to precisely describe an entrepreneur, by now you probably realize that today any definition of the term combines facets of all the earlier ones. Creator, innovator, promoter and marketer, risk-taker, decision-maker, organizer, special type of manager, reallocator of resources, leader, and proprietor—whatever you call them, entrepreneurs are here to stay. Here's a bit about what it takes to be a successful entrepreneur in the twenty-first century.

Entrepreneurs Are Made, Not Born

Ever since the eighteenth century, taking risks has been considered a fundamental attribute of the entrepreneur. Those risks have included life and limb as well as money. It's a myth that all entrepreneurs take big chances with their (or other people's) money. The intelligent ones don't. Instead, they take calculated risks based on past experience, research, and good judgment. But the fact that they take risks and can handle a lot more uncertainty than the rest of us doesn't mean they thrive on chaos. Most are very well organized—they have to be.

It's another myth that entrepreneurs are just lucky. More than likely, they've done their homework, have a good idea, and recognize a great opportunity when they see one. The rest of us usually see it only after it's been pointed out to us. If that's luck, then it's luck that they've generated themselves.

In addition to risk-takers, here are other kinds of people who make good entrepreneurs.

Excellent Communicators

There are few jobs that require no communication skills at all, and if you are the heart, soul, and face of your operation, then it behooves you to be a superlative communicator. Customers, clients, colleagues, and vendors alike need to know exactly what you want, and you need to know what they want. Pay attention to their answers, expectations, needs, and signals, and try to see things from their perspective. Listen to opposing ideas—you might learn something.

Smart Decision-Makers

Everyone makes decisions every day, but an entrepreneur has to make smart decisions and come up with solutions, ideas, and alternatives based on the information available at that moment and then put them into action. You may never have the leisure of researching your facts to death to make the absolutely, positively correct decision. If the answer you choose isn't quite right, try the next one. There are no perfect conditions for work, or life, for that matter. You will always have to do the best you can with the resources you have in the time allotted.

Multitaskers

You have to be willing to try new things and do many different tasks—even ones you don't like. It helps to be a quick study, too. There will be times when no one else is available to help, from designing an ad to compiling a spreadsheet to boxing up the product for shipping. That's when you learn how to do it yourself or find someone who can help you. If you want to do only one part of the business—for example, you love to sell to customers or craft the widgets with your own two hands—perhaps you should consider finding an employer who appreciates your special talents.

Team Builders

It's a romantic myth that all entrepreneurs are experts or go it alone. Think of William Hewlett and David Packard. Yes, they built a business empire out of some ideas they tinkered with in their garage, but they also established, promoted, and put their name on a business culture that valued teams, innovation, and fairness. Besides being a good leader and something of a visionary, an entrepreneur benefits from knowing how to assemble a great team of people whose skills and knowledge complement her own. The chances are good that there will be an expert or two in the group. If you can encourage a team of dedicated partners to rally around you, then think of the success you'll have with your clients.

Passionate Advocates

Some people downplay the relevance of passion in business in favor of the more pragmatic skills mentioned previously. But if you aren't passionate about what you are doing, how can you expect others to be? Passion about a service or product, like good humor, is infectious and will rub off on your colleagues. Some people think that money is the only thing that motivates entrepreneurs, but more often it's the chance to institute change or achieve a goal that is the more powerful motivator.

Entrepreneurial Qualities

There are many qualities that make a person suitable for one job and not another. Entrepreneurs are no different from you in that each one has his or her unique values, personality traits, interests, and skills. However, there are several characteristics that the more successful entrepreneurs seem to share. If you see yourself in this list, perhaps you have what it takes to become one.

Results- and Action-Oriented

Getting things done is the name of the game. As an entrepreneur, you may not have a staff or even one other person to whom you can hand projects. It's your name on the door, so you need to meet your deadlines. It's going to take planning, prioritizing, problem-solving, and proceeding. If these skills aren't your strong suits, you'll have to learn them or rethink your entrepreneurial plan.

Business and Personal Vision

It is very important that you have a vision for your business from start-up to exit strategy. You may not yet know how you're going to build it, but you need to know clearly what business you want to create. Why are you embarking on this venture? Your personal vision provides the foundation upon which you will construct your business. Writing down a one-sentence statement that you can refer to periodically can help you refocus if your efforts get off track.

Drive and Determination

Being an entrepreneur is a lot of work. If you don't have the internal drive to make your vision a reality, you won't get it from anywhere else. The going will get tough—that's a given. Your dedication to your vision (look at that statement you wrote down and taped over your desk) and self-motivation will be the qualities that keep you working hard in the face of the inevitable obstacles. Setting and achieving goals will propel you forward, but drive will give you momentum. Expect to work long hours. Some entrepreneurs are workaholics, but not all. A 2004 survey, reported on *www.Startup Journal.com*, noted that only 2 percent of the entrepreneurs asked would find it so hard to take time away from work that they'd have to call the office hourly.

Self-Confidence

Entrepreneurship is no place for shrinking violets. Unshakable confidence in your abilities and vision will stand you in good stead in all manner of circumstances. Remember those core values you identified in Chapter 2? Here is one way you can put them to good use. Customers, employees, and even competitors will respond more positively to you when you exhibit authentic confidence. Think about walking into a roomful of strangers, staffing a booth at a business convention, or making cold calls. Do you have the self-confidence to sell the public on your ideas?

Flexibility

This quality harkens back to good decision-making and comes from a combination of originality, curiosity, and analysis. If you can troubleshoot, generate lots of ideas, change plans quickly, and stay open to learning new things, you'll be prepared for the unexpected. On occasion you must even be prepared to give up your pet ideas, or "murder your darlings," as one pundit put it, in order to keep your eye on ultimate success. Entrepreneurs aren't usually just looking for that next hit-it-out-of-the-ballpark invention or breakthrough. What most of them come up with are tweaks and improvements. As Jeff Cornwall of the Center for Entrepreneurship says, "Hit for average, not for home runs!"

Optimism

It's highly unlikely that anyone would venture into the realm of the entrepreneur without a larger-than-healthy dose of optimism. The woe-is-me types aren't going to have much luck selling their ideas to willing customers. Most entrepreneurs are highly motivated to succeed before the ink is dry on their business plan. They can already envision their success and smell it in the air. The path to any worthwhile goal is going to encounter obstacles and setbacks—just like life. There won't be crowds of adoring fans tossing roses and accolades your way (although there might be a few of those). There may even be times when you doubt the wisdom of your decisions. Optimism will help you be patient and resilient. Many, if not most, successful entrepreneurs had at least one failed business before they made it big. In the culture of Silicon Valley, "failure" is worn as a badge of honor. Many people think that entrepreneurs worth their salt have to fail at something before they'll be taken seriously. Optimism means that you view mistakes not as failures but as steps in your learning process. Optimism also means that if you do fail, it was the strategy, product, or technique that failed, not you. If your idea didn't catch on, there is probably a better solution out there that you wouldn't have looked for otherwise.

Entrepreneurial Readiness Test

Your answers to the following questions will help you determine whether or not you're ready to take the plunge into business ownership.

1.	Are you comfortable with not receiving a regular paycheck?	☐ YES	☐ NO
2.	Do you like work that offers challenge, change, and variety, even if it involves some risk?	☐ YES	☐ NO
3.	Are you flexible enough to meet changing market demands?	☐ YES	☐ NO

4. Are you willing to invest your own money as well as ask others to invest in your business venture?	☐ YES	☐ NO
5. Are you committed to spending as much time and effort as it takes to make your business successful?	☐ YES	☐ NO
6. Is it important to you to do the strategic planning as well as take care of the day-to-day details of running a business?	☐ YES	☐ NO
7. Is your business idea based on your expertise, interests, and solid market research?	☐ YES	☐ NO
8. Are you able to bounce back and learn from failures or temporary setbacks?	☐ YES	☐ NO
9. Are you optimistic, persistent, and passionate about your work?	☐ YES	☐ NO
10. Are you confident that you are capable of succeeding as an entrepreneur?	☐ YES	☐ NO

Write this score on your chart on page 179.　　**My Yes Total** _____

Test developed by Susan Urquart-Brown. Material excerpted from *The Accidental Entrepreneur: Practical Wisdom for People Who Never Expected to Work for Themselves*, by Susan Urquart-Brown, found at www.TheAccidentalEntrepreneur.biz.

Scoring Your Test

8 to 10: You're ready to move ahead. If you answered "yes" to eight or more questions, you're ready to work seriously toward starting your own business. You are willing and able to take calculated risks that are based on experience and supported by solid information. You are probably energized by the work you do because you find it stimulating and innovative and it offers you opportunities to master new challenges. You are an independent thinker who is willing to listen to the advice of others, but you prefer to make your own decisions. However, don't launch your new enterprise too fast. Be sure to write down your business plan, including a marketing plan and some best-case/worst-case financial projections. Poor planning is one of the most common causes of business failure.

5 to 7: Move ahead slowly. If you answered "yes" to five to seven questions, you have some of the key entrepreneurial characteristics, but you need to move ahead slowly. Assess your strengths and weaknesses, and determine what you need to develop before you start a business. You might consider buying a franchise or an existing business instead of starting a business from scratch. You might also test your mettle by starting your business part-time, while working for someone else full- or part-time. Grow your business slowly. Only give up your employment when your own business grows large enough to be viable.

0 to 4: Consider working for someone else. If you answered "yes" to four or fewer of the questions, you would probably be more comfortable working for someone else. You're not yet confident of your ability to be your own boss and do what it takes to run a business. Perhaps you are interested in starting a business because you love delivering a particular service or making a product. If so, you might consider working for a company that values and fosters the entrepreneurial spirit or join a start-up team within a larger company. However, if you really want to start your own business, your determination can compensate for not having all of the entrepreneurial characteristics. Of course, if you have business partners you trust, a solid business idea, lots of capital, and have evaluated the financial prospects carefully, you just might want to go for it. But if you've really decided that entrepreneurship isn't for you, skip to Chapter 10 and test your managerial ability.

Overcoming Your Fear

Taking the plunge to start your own business can be scary. If your test score indicates that you are definitely interested in becoming an entrepreneur but you still have some trepidation, here are some things to consider to help you get beyond the fear.

Take Your Time

You don't have to start immediately. It takes time to plan, and once you start your business, it takes time to build it up. On average, it takes between three and five years to build a solid, successful, profitable business. Make a plan, set your goals, and take one step at a time.

Have Faith

Marketing and selling your product or service is much easier if you believe in yourself. Base your business on your core values, interests, strongest skills, and expertise.

Know Your Audience

Understand your market. Perception, experience, and savvy will help you hone in on and explore that niche just waiting to be occupied by you and your idea. Any investors you attract will want to feel confident that you have your finger on the pulse of your market.

Use Your Network

You don't have to do it all alone. Get support from your friends and family and advice from business professionals, coaches, and colleagues. Take advantage of community resources wherever you can find them. Don't fall into the trap of being the "lone wolf." This is a common mistake new entrepreneurs make. Ask for help when you need it because, in the long run, it will save you time and money.

Have a Solid Business Plan

Planning for battle or charting a course—pick your analogy. The important thing is that you have a well-crafted plan. Potential investors will notice and appreciate the facts on risk, return, and demand. Remember that most companies fail, so do everything you can to make yours one of the ones that doesn't. In many cases, sound implementation can count for more than a great idea.

Using Your Results

There are lots of ways to use your entrepreneurial skills. Some but not all of them involve leaving your job, selling a product, or making money. Here are some other ways you can feed your inner entrepreneur wherever you are.

Entre-Boomers

Baby Boomers have not only flouted the rules of the past few decades, they've torn them up and rewritten them. They're doing the same now to their parents' ideas about retirement. Rather than golf or cruises, a good number of them are looking into entrepreneurial pursuits to fill their golden years. A 2005 Challenger, Gray & Christmas survey found that 13 percent of the 3,000 job seekers polled had started their own business in the second quarter of their lives and 86.6 percent of those were over forty years old. U.S. Department of Labor figures show that one of the fastest groups of self-employed workers is age fifty-five and over. Boomers make up 54 percent of all self-employed workers outside agriculture, a 29 percent increase over the year 2000. Whether the catalyst for midlife entrepreneurship is suddenly getting laid off, a desire to help adult children financially, or simply being too full of energy and ideas to hang up the old briefcase, there's no question that it takes a lot of work and commitment. You may enjoy sewing outfits for your dog, but that doesn't mean you should turn your craft into a full-fledged business. The same qualities and qualifiers that apply to younger entrepreneurs apply to Boomers, too.

Intrapreneurs

Depending on your results on this test, you may come to realize that your talents and temperament are better suited to working within an organization and not on your own. That doesn't mean that you don't have entrepreneurial qualities or that you can't bring some of that spirit into your workplace as an "intrapreneur." Some ideas that can bring out the entrepreneur in every employee include the following:

- Have a fair process for screening and eliminating ideas.
- Decentralize the decision-making.
- Recognize and reward innovators and the managers who clear the way for innovation.
- Encourage free and open discussions of new ideas.
- Understand the unpredictable and sometimes disordered nature of innovation.

Post-It notes are a bit of "intrapreneurship" history. A 3M researcher invented the adhesive in 1968, but he was trying to come up with something completely different. Six years later, an innovative colleague came up with the idea of using the sticky stuff for bookmarks that wouldn't fall out of his church hymnal. Can you imagine life without Post-Its? Back in the 1960s, that original researcher probably thought his glue was a "failure."

Micropreneurs

A micropreneur is someone who takes on the risks and opportunities of a typical entrepreneur but who operates an extremely small business, typically with fewer than five employees. These businesses can be home-based and are frequently in industries that deal with knowledge, creativity, and/or information. A micropreneur might even operate two or more small businesses simultaneously. In 2002, Daniel H. Pink estimated in *Free Agent Nation* that there were 13 million micropreneurs in the United States. According to U.S. Census Bureau figures for 2000, 70 percent of businesses in the United States have no employees.

Social Entrepreneurs

You don't have to compromise your values in order to be an entrepreneur. You can be ambitious yet not focused solely on profit. Social entrepreneurs don't want to just throw money at society's ills. These "compassionate capitalists" want to find ways to apply their risk-taking, results-oriented business savvy to no less of a challenge than effecting societal change. The idea isn't new—Florence Nightingale and Maria Montessori transformed nursing and education 100 and more years ago—but it's no longer just the purview of single-minded idealists. As the concept gathers momentum, new humanitarian industries, agencies, and educational institutions are springing up around the world. One of them is the Skoll Foundation in Palo Alto, California. Jeff Skoll, a founder of eBay, knows something about entrepreneurship. He became an engineer, but even as a teenager he knew he wanted to make a difference. Now, armed with a Stanford MBA and a fortune worth several billion dollars, he chairs a foundation that grants millions to support innovative approaches to the resolution of social issues around the world. In 2003, the foundation established the Centre for Social Entrepreneurship at Oxford University to teach the concepts to young visionaries-in-the-making. As Cheryl Dahle writes in *Fast Company* (*www.fastcompany.com*),

"What defines entrepreneur . . . is that relentless problem-solving approach, not the specifics of the problem itself."

As you fill in your test results on the chart on pages 178–179, your values, interests, skills, and personality, along with such needs as autonomy and independence, will tell you whether or not entrepreneurship is right for you. If you think you have the traits of an entrepreneur, go for it! If you don't have all of them now, you can develop them if you want it badly enough. Just remember the immortal words of Yogi Berra: "When you see a fork in the road, take it!"

Chapter 10

Managerial Suitability and Your Career

Perhaps you're thinking that you have been the low person on the work totem pole long enough and it's time to move up. You have great rapport with your coworkers. You know what it takes to get the job done. The results of your personality, skills, and entrepreneurial abilities tests lead you to believe you'd be a great manager. You may be right. The test in this chapter will help you decide if you have what it takes to be the boss.

10

What Is a Manager?

There are many types and levels of managers, but generally, a manager is the link between upper management and employees. A manager is responsible for overseeing the work of others and for achieving company objectives. Managers have control over resources, schedules, and expenditures, among other things. As a manager rather than a staffperson, you have more power to exert changes within your organization and help direct its growth. By virtue of their position, managers wield a certain amount of power and influence. Just how they wield that power determines whether they are successful or inadequate managers.

Not all successful managers are alike. They differ in the ways they go about their work or the type of environment they prefer. Some like a fast pace and rapid changes; others like organized structure and set systems. Many thrive on challenges or creativity. One thing successful managers do seem to share, however, is that they get along with people. Your results on your skills, personality, and emotional intelligence tests in Chapters 3, 5, and 11 will help you figure out if you are a people person, but you probably already have a pretty good idea whether you are or not by the types of activities and work situations you enjoy.

While there are many types and styles, managers in every organization share some basic duties and qualities, such as the following.

Managers Plan, Organize, Prioritize, and Budget

People in managerial positions are called upon to plan projects and meetings, decide who does what when, know when ends have been achieved, and establish and stick to budgets. A good manager can organize the maelstrom of papers, e-mails, telephone calls, meetings, and directives that flood one's desk on any given day by keeping priorities straight. By setting clear goals for projects, people, the organization, and oneself, you can tell when you've achieved success.

Managers Analyze, Evaluate, Delegate, and Take Action

The ability to identify a problem, consider solutions, set realistic goals, come up with strategies for attaining them, and assign tasks and responsibilities to the right people is a hallmark of a good manager. The boss also needs to be able to evaluate the skills, knowledge, and abilities of staff; monitor project status and work progress; and do what's needed to achieve goals and meet deadlines.

Large projects can't be done by one person. Managers know what to delegate, how to delegate, and to whom to delegate in order to get the job done effectively. Being able to delegate well frees up a manager's time to do all those other things she does that earn the big salary. Because they've prioritized their work, managers can take action to produce results for the company and solve problems ranging from employee grievances to project snags. A manager who is holed up in an office bemoaning an unsympathetic superior or lack of support, or playing the victim, is unlikely to be able to spur his employees to new heights of achievement or recognize if conflicts are brewing in the office. Proactive managers can get to the root of a problem before it becomes a bigger issue. They take responsibility for their lives, their work, and the results of their actions, and they encourage their staff to do the same.

Managers Communicate Well

You can't fake this. One gripe frequently heard around workplaces is that staff members feel out of the loop about what's going on in the company, especially in times of upheaval or layoffs. A manager who keeps employees informed and answers their questions honestly will let them know how they fit into the big picture and keep them committed to the enterprise.

Nobody expects all managers to write like Shakespeare or hold forth like Winston Churchill, but a certain aptitude with words goes a long way toward achieving desired ends. If you can express yourself clearly, you reduce the chance for error when others interpret your words.

Managers are often called upon to run meetings with one person or dozens of people and perhaps present papers or reports to an audience of hundreds. For most people, death is less terrifying than speaking in public. Join an organization, sign up for a seminar, or take some training in the art of public speaking so you can remain calm, cool, and collected in front of an audience, whether of staff, your superiors, or a roomful of strangers. Managers who can't speak well in front of a group lose credibility.

Is there a career that requires no writing whatsoever? Probably not, and many require a great deal of it in the form of reports, staff or project evaluations, presentations, agendas, summaries, briefs, and memos, to name a few. Part of a manager's responsibility is to communicate the company and department's mission, responsibilities, policies, procedures, and job information and expectations to staff members, whether in person or in writing. Good, clear writing is like any other skill—you can learn how to do it with practice. There are myriad resources to help you, from books to workshops. Enlist an assistant or associate to help edit and proofread, especially for the important documents. Everyone needs a second set of eyes to catch those dangling participles and misplaced modifiers.

Perhaps the preceding are some of the skills you identified in yourself in Chapter 3. Not all people can be good managers—nor should they be managers. The philosopher Friedrich Nietzsche noted, "Whoever does not know how to hit the nail on the head should not be asked to hit it at all."

Good Managers Are Made, Not Born

According to an August 2005 Gallup poll, 80 percent of the working adults surveyed were somewhat or completely satisfied with their bosses or immediate supervisors (*www.gallup.com*). Those managers are doing something right. Good managers are responsible for the same types of tasks as mediocre managers, but they accomplish them more effectively and efficiently while maintaining good professional relationships along the way. The stars also possess some special skills that make them stand out.

Good Managers Build Teams, Mentor, and Empower Workers

Teamwork is essential to most types of work these days. Helping teams collaborate and achieve their goals is one of a good manager's strongest qualities. It may require you to check your ego at the door for the good of the group, too. Learn how to lead brainstorming sessions, listen to everyone's input, and follow through.

A good manager trusts her employees and gives them the freedom to ask questions and take responsibility for their own work. Management consultant Marcus Buckingham says, "Bad managers play checkers. Good managers play chess" (*http://knowledge.wharton.upenn.edu*). A good manager identifies and capitalizes on the unique skills of each worker and will defer to employees in their areas of expertise and responsibility. Sir Howard Stringer, chairman and CEO of Sony Corporation, admitted in a June 2006 issue of *The New Yorker*, "I'm very happy to delegate. . . . I really do rely upon people who know a lot more than I do."

Rather than feeling threatened by rising stars in their departments, a good manager takes the time to coach or mentor others, secure in the knowledge that their successes will reflect favorably on him. Rich Moore of AAIM Management Association says, "If you don't develop your people, you have nothing" (*www.ccfbest.org*).

Good managers know when to give help, when to ask for it, and when to accept it when it's offered.

Good Managers Lead, Motivate, and Reward

Managers can't make anyone do anything; all they can do is ask. The good ones know how to do it without acting like a tyrant. One study mentioned in *How Full Is Your Bucket?* by Tom Rath and Donald O. Clifton (Gallup Press) found that health care employees who worked for a manager they disliked had significantly higher blood pressure. They estimate that negative and disengaged workers cost U.S. businesses hundreds of billions of dollars per year. A good manager doesn't look for ways to motivate employees but looks for ways to help employees motivate themselves. As Edward Deci writes in *Why We Do What We Do: Understanding Self-Motivation* (Penguin), people are self-motivated in places where they feel connected, autonomous, and competent. Managers can encourage risk-taking and creativity, accept failure as part of the process, and find new ways for employees to be successful. Harvard Medical School psychologist Dr. Robert Brooks came up with the notion of "islands of competence," which he says everyone has (*www.drrobertbrooks.com*). When a manager focuses on reinforcing these in an employee, rather than just trying to correct perceived problems or weaknesses, the employee can feel more pride and achievement. The skills and interests that you discovered in Chapters 3 and 4 should help you find a career that uses your "islands of competence."

Good managers inspire and motivate their workers by not trying to shoe-horn them all into the same mold. Instead, they endeavor to discover each employee's strengths and fit him or her with suitable tasks at which to excel. When an employee feels a personal stake in his work, he will feel responsible for the work, motivated to perform well, and resilient in the face of setbacks. Good leaders have standards, live up to them, and expect their staff to do the same. A study conducted at Johnson & Johnson in the late 1990s indicated that high-performing leaders scored highest in emotional intelligence (see Chapter 11), including such competencies as self-confidence, initiative, drive, and adaptability (*www.eiconsortium.org*). This and other studies found no evidence to suggest that men and women differ in leadership effectiveness.

A good leader knows when to collaborate, when to step back and let someone else shine, and also when to take charge. President Woodrow Wilson noted, "Leadership does not always wear the harness of compromise." Sometimes you have to take the bull by the horns and own responsibility for the outcome.

U.S. Department of Labor data show that the main reason people leave their jobs is that they don't feel appreciated. Don't miss a chance to praise the good work of your staff—and share credit for goals accomplished and projects completed. Encouraging employees' unique contributions helps them feel successful and motivated. Remember from Chapter 8 that money isn't the only way to reward your staff. The variety of incentives is practically infinite, from a simple "thank you" to a bonus to a paid sabbatical. Don't forget that contributions come in many shapes and sizes, too. Rather than always rewarding the person with the most sales, recognize the people who innovate new strategies to improve customer relations or whose quality of work has improved markedly, even if they aren't the top sellers.

Good Managers Listen, Cope, and Persevere

The exceptional managers have high emotional intelligence (EI; see Chapter 11). Listening, coping, self-awareness, and persevering are hallmarks of EI.

The late politician Dean Rusk said, "One of the best ways to persuade others is with your ears—by listening to them." A manager who doesn't truly listen to employees won't earn the respect of those employees or even truly know what's going on in the organization.

A confident, self-aware, and proactive manager is not one who succumbs to stress, frustration, or anger at every little setback. She may feel the pressure, but she doesn't use it as an excuse to call employees on the carpet, blame others for her own mistakes, or crumble in difficult times. These managers don't retreat from challenges but have the drive and creativity to approach problems from different directions and learn from mistakes. They also know when they should cut their losses and abandon a goal.

People who know their own strengths and weaknesses know how to perform in a productive and not a self-defeating way. Self-aware managers can help their staff tap into their own strengths and weaknesses.

Good Managers Are Flexible and Focused

From layoffs to mergers to acquisitions, managers need to be able to adapt—and thrive—in a climate of change. Martin Yate and Peter Sander note in *Knock 'em Dead Management* (Adams Media) that the pace of business is faster than ever before. "Managers who stay on top of change and anticipate it are more highly regarded than managers who seem to be consumed by change and are always playing catchup." What they term "change-awareness" is a skill highly valued by employers.

Good managers operate with a steady moral, professional, emotional compass. They don't blow every which way the wind blows but bend when necessary and stay flexible enough to adjust to changing circumstances.

Work expert Gloria Mark at the University of California–Irvine has studied workplace interruptions. One of her suggestions: If you can't handle interruptions, don't become a manager. The average amount of time spent on any single task before being interrupted is about three minutes. Anyone incapable of limiting interruptions or getting back to work after an interruption isn't going to be able to stay focused and manage time and other people well (*http://gmj.gallup.com*).

Good Managers Are . . . Moms?

A May 2005 study by a women's networking organization found that 69 percent of employees surveyed would rather work for a mother than a woman who is not a mother, citing mothers' skills at prioritizing, motivating, and patience (*www.usatoday.com*). You don't need to rush out and have a child in order to improve your management skills, but borrowing a few ideas from what moms do well couldn't hurt.

Managerial Suitability Test

Remember that not everyone is cut out to be a manager. While it takes a certain set of skills and knowledge to perform a job, it takes different skills to manage other people well. This test will help you determine if you have what it takes to become a manager.

Read each statement and decide how much it sounds like you. If it sounds like you often, score 3; sometimes, score 2; and rarely, score 1. Remember, there are no right or wrong answers.

1. _____ I have the ability to find key issues in a situation.
2. _____ I am known for getting my points across effectively.
3. _____ I am interested in the growth and development of others.
4. _____ I am good at organizing myself and managing my time.
5. _____ I have a good sense of priorities.
6. _____ I communicate my feelings as well as my ideas.
7. _____ I like to motivate others to achieve a common task.
8. _____ I set a good example in my work.
9. _____ I am able to think things through and make key decisions.
10. _____ People know where I stand on important issues.
11. _____ I make it a priority to help others succeed at work.
12. _____ I adapt easily to changes around me.
13. _____ I am able to analyze, synthesize, and value a situation.
14. _____ I am able to clearly define the tasks at hand.
15. _____ I am good at building the synergy of a team.
16. _____ I maintain high standards of personal performance.
17. _____ I can find new ways to overcome a problem.
18. _____ I know when to appropriately use humor to relieve tension.

19. _____ I am able to give others a sense that they are doing something worthwhile.

20. _____ I am willing to accept the risks of leadership.

21. _____ I am able to assess consequences.

22. _____ I am comfortable giving honest feedback to others.

23. _____ I am able to take the initiative to get a group going.

24. _____ I have a sense of pride in my own work.

25. _____ I can evaluate team performance.

26. _____ I am tactful and sensitive when dealing with others.

27. _____ I like to inspire and encourage others.

28. _____ I am curious about people, ideas, and things.

29. _____ I evaluate myself and my work on an ongoing basis.

30. _____ I am good at asking for input and listening to others.

31. _____ I am able to recognize qualities and abilities and give credit to others.

32. _____ I am known for fair dealing and honesty.

33. _____ I know how my work contributes to the overall result.

34. _____ I am able to give clear, concise directions to others.

35. _____ I like to get to know, encourage, and motivate others.

36. _____ I have an open mind in respect to others' points of view.

37. _____ I set realistic and challenging targets.

38. _____ I treat others with dignity and respect.

39. _____ I can effectively delegate the tasks at hand.

40. _____ I can be a stabilizing influence in a crisis.

41. _____ I operate well under pressure or in a rapidly changing environment.

42. _____ I encourage and listen to new ideas.

43. _____ I like to motivate others by understanding their needs and aspirations.

44. _____ I can effectively deal with stress.

45. _____ I am able to set goals and measure progress toward them.

46. _____ I pay close attention to others when they are speaking.

47. _____ I like to give personal guidance and direction.

48. _____ I can face up to a mistake and not blame others.

Scoring Your Test

Record your score for each numbered statement in the following spaces.

Vision

These indicate your ability to understand the big picture, the direction of the organization, and goals of the project.

_____ 1

_____ 5

_____ 9

_____ 13

_____ 17

_____ 21

_____ 25

_____ 29

_____ 33

_____ 37

_____ 41

_____ 45

_____ Vision Subtotal (out of a possible 36)

Communication Skills

These indicate your ability to write, speak, and listen effectively.

_____ 2

_____ 6

_____ 10

_____ 14

_____ 18

_____ 22

_____ 26

_____ 30

_____ 34

_____ 38

_____ 42

_____ 46

_____ Communication Skills Subtotal (out of a possible 36)

Motivation of Others

These indicate your ability to encourage and inspire employees to achieve goals and objectives.

_____ 3
_____ 7
_____ 11
_____ 15
_____ 19
_____ 23
_____ 27
_____ 31
_____ 35
_____ 39
_____ 43
_____ 47
_____ Motivation Subtotal (out of a possible 36)

Self-Awareness

These indicate the strength of your sense of your own capabilities and place within the organizational structure.

_____ 4
_____ 8
_____ 12
_____ 16
_____ 20
_____ 24
_____ 28
_____ 32
_____ 36
_____ 40
_____ 44
_____ 48
_____ Self-Awareness Subtotal (out of a possible 36)

Score Totals

_____ Now add up your subtotals and write your total score here (out of a possible 144) and on the chart on page 179. Also note on the chart your two highest-scoring areas (Vision, Communication Skills, Motivation of Others, or Self-Awareness).

If you scored a total of 100 or more, you are probably well suited to be a manager, but take the time to reflect on the areas in which you scored lowest to see potential areas for growth.

If you scored between 60 and 100, being a manager may be appropriate for you, but find out more about what is required.

If you scored below 60, managing others is probably not for you, at least not at this point in your career. You may be happiest as an individual contributor.

No matter how you scored on this test, your answers probably indicate one or two areas that you could improve. Note them here and on the chart on page 179.

Areas for Growth

_____

_____

Using Your Results

Moving into a managerial position from a staff position is a big step. It's one you may want to undertake to expand your business skills, earn higher pay, or gain more satisfaction from your career. Know that your day-to-day tasks will change. If you once worked in solitude on well-defined projects, reporting only to your boss, as a manager your day will be filled with much more interaction with others, scheduling, planning, and, of course, meetings.

Just as you can pick up the skills necessary for your chosen career, you can learn how to be a manager, too. As noted previously, good managers are made, not born. Experience and training will help you develop your managerial skills. Look into some of these options.

- Seminars and conferences conducted by organizations, such as the American Management Association (*www.amanet.org*), cover the gamut of management topics.
- College classes from big-name schools such as the Stanford Graduate School of Business (*www.gsb.stanford.edu*) or from your local community college can give you the expertise you need.
- If your company offers it, in-house management training is a resource you should take advantage of, if management is your goal.
- Find a mentor. Make sure you find someone in the workplace who is an extremely good manager to be your mentor.
- Online resources, such as the Gallup Management Journal (*http://gmj.gallup.com*), The Wharton School at the University of Pennsylvania (*http://knowledge.wharton.upenn.edu*), or self-tutoring books, such as *Knock 'em Dead Management: The Ultimate Guide to Managing People, Setting Goals, and Achieving Success* by Martin Yate and Peter Sander (Adams Media) or *One-Minute Manager* by Kenneth Blanchard and Spencer Johnson (Berkeley Trade) offer valuable advice from experts.
- Use your own experience in the workplace to guide your career as a manager. Everyone who has worked for any length of time has had both good and bad managers. Think about the traits you want to emulate, as well as the ones to disregard.

How to Be a Bad Manager

Think that people leave their jobs because they want more money? A 2001 study found that the number one reason people left was "poor supervisory behavior" (*www.microsoft.com*). Another poll found that, given the chance, 21 percent of employees would fire their bosses (*www.andreakay.com*). Jeffrey Kluger wrote about ambition and success in *Time* magazine, noting, "Grand dreams unmoored from morals are the stuff of tyrants" (November 14, 2005). Studies of high-achieving college students and any examination of the corporate implosions of recent years reveal that many ambitious people in high-stress situations suffer distorted views of success and themselves. Some resort to cheating and other unethical or immoral behavior to achieve their desired ends. Here's how to follow in their foot-steps.

A bad manager:

- **Does it all.** Nobody knows the work like you do. If you delegate some portion of it to someone else, that person is bound to mess it up. Anyway, if someone else did do a good job on something, your boss might notice and take some responsibility away from you. If you have to delegate, dole out the mindless drudgery or make sure that everyone has to come to you for approval before they make one decision, no matter how minor.

- **Hogs the credit.** Make sure your boss knows that you completed that project single-handedly and that all those brilliant ideas were yours and yours alone. If your staff protests, threaten them into silence. After all, you deserve that big promotion. Yes, it is all about you.

- **Punishes mistakes.** You expect your staff to be perfect. Let them know that taking risks is bad. You told them it was a lame idea in the first place, didn't you? Make them feel ashamed for even trying. Punishment builds character.

- **Reprimands in public.** Wait until the next staff meeting to ream out an underling for incompetence. You're sure everyone will agree with you, and the miscreant needs to be taught a lesson.

- **Is heartless.** Call David "Fred," ignore birthdays, and dock the pay of the woman who missed two days because of her husband's surgery. Treat your workers as drones with no personal lives or responsibilities. After all, bees are highly efficient workers, and they don't need to know everyone's name in the hive. But they do know who the queen bee is. Use intimidation to get your way. Mollycoddling is for weaklings.

- **Is isolated.** Close your door so that no one can come to you with questions, problems, or their petty personal issues. Post a "Keep Out!" sign for good measure. You don't have time to wander around making yourself available to every Tom, Dick, or Nancy.

- **Is aloof.** An air of aloofness will keep your staff from bringing up sensitive issues or difficulties. Intimidating them will also forestall their interacting with you in any way, thereby giving you more time to get your work done. You deserve respect because of your position. If you can get them to call you "Your Highness," so much the better.

- **Admits no mistakes.** You believe managers should be perfect—you certainly are—and you have all the answers. If by some chance you do make a mistake, find someone on whom to pin the blame. In that way, you won't tarnish your appearance of infallibility. What's important is being right. Being sorry is for suckers.

- **Tunes others out.** Sometimes it sounds like so much yada, yada, yada. Nobody can possibly know as much about the project as you do, so continue typing that e-mail or shuffling those papers until the person stops talking and goes away. Certainly don't ask for anyone's input on major decisions.

- **Gives unclear direction.** Say one thing and do another. Listen to the last person you talked to, then change your mind when someone new comes up with a different idea. It will keep your employees on their toes. Let your mantra be: "Just get it done." If no one completely understands what you want, how can they tell you it's wrong? Assume they get it. Anyway, even if they don't, you can chew them out later for messing up. It's a win-win situation.

- **Micromanages.** If you do delegate some small portion of the work to someone else, make sure you scrutinize every aspect of it. Be prepared to stay up late redoing everything they've done because it's probably wrong.

- **Lies.** Tell your staff what they want to hear to shut them up, but keep the real information to yourself, especially the bad news. They couldn't handle the truth. Besides, warning them of impending layoffs only takes their attention away from the work.

- **Ignores the deadwood.** There's too much paperwork involved in getting rid of those nonperformers. Keeping them on makes your department look bigger. If you had to let them go, who knows if you could replace them?

- **Is serious.** Humor has no place in the office. You have responsibilities, and levity is an unwelcome distraction. Work is serious business. Wipe that smile off your face.

A Manager Is a Work in Progress

Some call managing an art form. Certainly it is a multifaceted skill that requires practice. Not everyone wants to do it, not everyone can do it, and even fewer can do it extremely well. Know that becoming a manager isn't going to happen overnight. It's unlikely that you'll be promoted straight from typist to head of a department. Rather, it's more likely to be an incremental process whereby you assume more and more responsibility, figure out how to delegate tasks, and learn the ropes gradually, progressively, and systematically. If you're lucky enough to have a mentoring manager yourself, you're in good hands. Learning how to manage is kind of like learning how to swim. If you have a good teacher, you won't get thrown into the deep end of the pool without a life preserver and told to paddle for your life—or drown. You'll have ample opportunity to test the waters in the shallow end. Before you know it, you'll be swimming like a pro.

Keep in mind that managing isn't for everyone—it may not even be right for you—nor is it the only way to get ahead in your career. Many enlightened companies, such as Charles Schwab and lots of high-tech firms, acknowledge and reward independent contributors just as they do managers. Once you've filled in your chart with the results from all of your tests, you'll know if becoming a manager is something you want to pursue.

Chapter 11

Emotional Intelligence and Your Career

You've got the smarts and skills. You know your interests. You try to live and work by your personal values. The office furniture is picked out in the location where you want to live. You've achieved a pretty fair balance between the demands of your workplace and obligations at home. Hold on. There's one more piece of the self-assessment puzzle yet to put in place. That piece is emotional intelligence, and it can play just as big a role in your career satisfaction as any quality you've tested so far.

What Is Emotional Intelligence?

Aristotle said, "Anyone can become angry—that is easy. But to be angry at the right person, to the right degree, at the right time, for the right purpose, and in the right way—that is not easy." Twenty-three hundred years ago the Greek philosopher already had a pretty good handle on emotional intelligence, and the field hadn't even been invented yet.

Simply put, emotional intelligence (EI, but sometimes referred to as EQ) refers to your ability to correctly identify, understand, manage, and learn from your own emotions and those of others and then act in ways that best serve your interests. In short, it means acting like an adult. Obviously, understanding and managing emotions is an important skill in your personal life. It's something that helps keep families happy. But here you are focusing on your career. Psychologist Daniel Goleman wrote in *Working with Emotional Intelligence* (Bantam) that "the rules for work are changing." These rules have nothing to do with your intellectual ability or technical skills—at many levels of achievement, those are a given. The new rules focus on "personal qualities, such as initiative and empathy, adaptability and persuasiveness." Those are all qualities that are intimately intertwined with emotional intelligence. It's hard to imagine the moguls of the past—the Leland Stanfords, Andrew Carnegies, or John D. Rockefellers—worrying about empathizing with their underlings, but today's workplace is a whole different animal.

The idea of emotional intelligence has captured corporate America's attention. The *Harvard Business Review* called EI nothing less than a "paradigm-shattering idea" for the business world. The research from the past decade is impressive: Emotional intelligence can help make the difference between a leader and a loser. In the late 1990s, an analysis of over 300 top-level executives from more than one dozen global companies identified the emotional competencies that set the stars apart, and they included influence, self-confidence, achievement drive, and leadership. One study estimated the annual cost to U.S. business of ignoring EI to be between $5.6 and $16.8 billion dollars (*www.eiconsortium.org*).

The power of EI comes from being the foundation upon which a person can build such emotional competencies. Those are the personal and social skills that keep you motivated and help you achieve goals. EI, not GPA, seems to fuel the success of the peak performer.

That's a pretty surprising statement, especially if you've never heard of emotional intelligence before. You undoubtedly know some emotionally intelligent people—you may be one yourself. They are the ones who are described as being great with people, particularly intuitive, or sure of exactly what they want and actively pursue it. Don't despair if you aspire to these qualities but don't feel you measure up; your EI score can be improved.

Different people have defined EI and its components in different ways, but for the purposes of the test in this chapter, you'll focus on five main areas: self-awareness, self-regulation, self-motivation, empathy, and social understanding.

Self-Awareness

This means that you know what emotions you're feeling and why, and you know how your feelings affect what you do, say, and think. Psychologist Erich Fromm said it was the quality that distinguished man from animal. Emotionally self-aware people don't ignore or obsess about their emotions. If someone seems to slight you at work or fails to return your calls, do you explode, try to ignore how you feel, or worry that you may have done something to antagonize him? If you're not careful, you can spend all your time fretting over nothing. Try to remember: It's not always about you. Repressing how you really feel doesn't make the whole issue go away, and blowing up only makes matters worse. If you possess healthy self-awareness, you know your strengths and weaknesses, can learn from experience, have a sense of perspective about yourself, and are self-confident and decisive.

Self-Regulation

This means you can manage your emotions in a positive way. A manager who explodes over every little problem or yells at a customer isn't going to reach his goals or win the respect and cooperation of his employees. In his book, *Emotional Intelligence* (Bantam), psychologist Daniel Goleman noted the shift in our culture from "Have a nice day!" to "Make my day!" These days, anything, no matter how trivial, seems to set people off. People feel disrespected, insulted, and maligned at the slightest provocation. A few years ago, a San Jose, California, man grabbed a woman's dog out of her car and threw it into oncoming traffic, where it died, all because she had bumped his fender in rush-hour traffic. This show of emotional incompetence landed the man in jail, where he presumably had plenty of time to contemplate his lack of EI and use the experience to foster his mental and emotional growth. Such out-of-proportion reactions are not only inappropriate, they're also scary and can be dangerous.

Self-regulation is another word for self-control. The playwright Oscar Wilde summed up a person lacking in self-regulation when he wrote, "I can resist everything, except temptation." People with good emotional self-control can delay gratification in favor of future goals or rewards. In the famous "marshmallow studies" by psychologist Walter Mischel at Stanford University, four-year-olds were asked to stay alone in a room with a marshmallow until the researcher came back. If the child resisted temptation, he or she could have two marshmallows when the researcher returned. Two-thirds of the children waited. Studies have shown that people who can delay gratification tend to be more successful than people who have no emotional self-regulation. They are the ones who can say "no" to a friend's all-night Alfred Hitchcock movie marathon in favor of working late to finish a big report. They're the ones who don't throw up their hands in defeat at the first sign of difficulty or opposition on a project, but instead buckle down and work out the problems. Top-level athletes exhibit a good sense of self-regulation. Challenges or stressful situations don't send these people off the deep end, which is an extremely useful skill to have in a high-pressure work environment.

Another aspect of self-regulation involves monitoring negative thoughts. Do you keep up a running interior (or spoken) monologue about how miserable your job is, how much you hate your coworkers, or how you wish your boss would just go away? Not only does it not help you, it can also poison your attitude, your motivation, and your relationships.

Just as you budget your money, you might also think of yourself as having an "emotional budget." If every trivial incident sends you into a rage, plunges you into despair, or fills you with euphoria, what will you have left in your emotional store for the events that really call for such feelings? Self-management means being able to gauge situations and respond with the appropriate emotions. If you can self-regulate your emotions, you can be more adaptable, conscientious, and open to new ideas.

Self-Motivation

This is one of the key elements of EI. It means that you are results-oriented, you can set goals and work toward them, even in the face of obstacles or setbacks, and you are always striving to improve. EI puts the "motion" in "emotion" through motivation. All three words come from the Latin *movere*, meaning "to move." Let's say you have to complete a long and difficult project. By imagining how good the project will be once you've worked hard on it, how proud you'll feel, and how happy your boss will be with you, you can garner the motivation to plunge into the work and stay focused. Self-motivation means taking responsibility for your emotions, decisions, and actions, as well as your mistakes and successes. Self-motivated people have a sense of purpose, initiative, and optimism.

Empathy

Empathy means that you are able to put yourself in the place of others and really understand what they are thinking, feeling, and experiencing. Scout Finch learned this lesson in *To Kill a Mockingbird* when Atticus told her, "You never really understand a person until you consider things from his point of view." Showing empathy is not the same as showing sympathy. Steven J. Stein and Howard E. Book distinguish the two in *The EQ Edge* (Wiley) as: "Empathetic statements begin with the word 'you'" and put the listener first. "Sympathetic statements begin with 'I' or 'my' and reflect the speaker's perspective."

Bullies lack empathy. Psychopaths lack empathy, being concerned only with their own self-interest. One criminal psychologist has come up with a Psychopathy Checklist. He maintains that some of the executives of the companies that failed so spectacularly in recent years would score as psychopathic, in other words, selfish and remorseless in their dealings with others, yet remarkably adept at reading and manipulating the feelings of others (*www.fastcompany.com*).

Empathy can help you understand the behavior of others, even if that behavior seems to contradict what they say. Empathy is invaluable in the workplace because it makes you a good listener, and it makes you better able to get along with and respect people whose opinions, experience, and background may differ from yours. Any job that requires customer contact will benefit from empathy. Empathetic people anticipate others' needs, offer assistance, and look for ways to increase customer satisfaction.

Social Understanding

This means that you can recognize emotions in others and use that understanding to effectively handle, build, and maintain relationships. In the workplace, you can accurately read social situations in order to persuade, lead, negotiate, avoid conflict, or settle disputes. This sort of awareness helps you recognize what other people are feeling based on clues, such as their facial expressions and body language, so that you can then put your understanding of the situation to use by steering it in a positive direction.

Do you remember from Chapter 3 what skills employers most wanted in employees (and often found lacking)? One of them was the ability to work in teams. An experiment at Yale University showed that an actor planted in a group assigned the task of determining bonuses for subordinates could infect the group with his emotion, whether cheerful, depressed, or hostile. A 2005 study by the Institute for Organizational Performance shows that "building strong relationships is a core leadership competency," according to Director Joshua Freedman (*www.eqperformance.com*). Research by the Center for Creative Leadership has shown that emotional incompetence derails workers more than any other factor. Poor interpersonal relations and the inability to work well in a team are two of the primary factors (*www.eiconsortium.org*). People with good social understanding can lead by example, handle difficult people tactfully, collaborate, and foster open communication.

EI Versus IQ

For decades, the IQ test was the accepted measure of human abilities. It seemed logical that verbal, mathematical, reasoning, and spatial skills would predict a person's future success. If you were smart, why wouldn't you do well in work and in life? But people with high IQs are by no means always the most successful. Who hasn't been in a situation when overthinking made it worse? Research has shown that IQ by itself isn't a very good predictor of job performance. Estimates of its value in measuring success vary from between 4 and 25 percent. There was obviously another piece to the puzzle, and that piece turned out to be emotional intelligence.

What Is IQ?

Many regard IQ as a genetically given "score," and nothing you can do or learn can change it. It's a different story for emotional intelligence. It would be disheartening to think that someone who lacked any degree of perseverance, empathy, or self-awareness now could never improve those competencies. Fortunately, research and practical applications of social and emotional learning have proven otherwise. Some consider emotional intelligence to be an innate potential, and by training it, you gain emotional competencies. Most agree that the skills associated with it are teachable and learnable. Certainly Redford and Virginia Williams do. In their book, *In Control* (Rodale), they maintain that people can learn to master such skills as remaining cool and calm in emotionally charged situations to the benefit of individuals, workplaces, and society in general.

IQ and EI are inexorably linked, of course, and research indicates that the latter actually helps the former. In studies of children and even of adult PhDs, who by definition possess a certain level of cognitive abilities, the results have shown that what made the biggest difference in how well they did later in life were their social and emotional abilities. Remember those kids in the "marshmallow studies"? Walter Mischel tracked down those same kids as teenagers and found that the two-thirds who waited for their treat at four years old scored remarkably higher on the SAT than the one-third who didn't.

EI Requires Contact

Emotional intelligence probably could be learned from books, but it isn't likely. Like values, one's emotional intelligence is learned through family relationships and behaviors, by interacting with other people on a daily basis and seeing how others act toward you. A child who spends most of his waking hours alone, communing with a computer, isn't going to have much opportunity to develop emotional competencies. Despite the popularity of e-mailing, online chat rooms, and instant messaging, they are pale substitutes for honest-to-goodness, face-to-face human contact. The emotions have yet to be invented that can convey all of the subtleties of human expression. A child who has plenty of opportunities to learn how to interpret her own feelings, interpret the way others are feeling, and understand how her actions affect other people is going to be able to develop a high emotional intelligence.

Today, many schools have programs in "social and emotional learning," or SEL. In many states, it's a required part of the curriculum, its proponents arguing that it's just as important to recognize one's own emotions and feel empathy for others as it is to construct legible sentences or balance a checkbook. It makes sense, too, especially if such programs can prevent bullying, violent behaviors, or drug abuse in favor of improved self-confidence and academic achievement.

A Short History of EI

Remember the old adage "There is nothing new under the sun"? It holds true for EI, too. The idea of emotional intelligence didn't emerge fully formed, like Athena from the head of Zeus. It evolved over many years as these things do, with researchers building upon the ideas of those before, often in disparate but related fields, until they converged into the concepts we recognize as EI today.

Nonverbal Emotional Expression

Charles Darwin shook things up with his theory of evolution, but almost twenty years after the publication of his *The Origin of Species,* he published *The Expression of the Emotions in Man and Animals* (1872). He found nonverbal expressions of fear, pleasure, anger, and other emotions in every living creature, even cows. He proposed that expressions were universal and inborn and that they had evolved over millennia. In his day, when the world was much smaller, people scoffed at the idea that a look of disgust in China would be recognizable to someone in England. Later research, of course, proved Darwin right.

In 1884, William James published "What Is an Emotion?" in the journal *Mind.* He recognized the body's connection to emotions, from flushed face to fidgeting to rapid breathing.

Repressed Emotions

Around the turn of the twentieth century, the Austrian psychologist Sigmund Freud understood that there was more to a person than rational thought. His insights helped make clear that human actions aren't always rational or logical. Freud built a practice helping people to recognize and release repressed emotions through a process called psychoanalysis. He recognized that people hide or disguise true feelings and believed that repressed emotions were the source of neurotic behavior.

Social Intelligence and Multiple Intelligence

In 1920s and 1930s, Robert Thorndike wrote about "different intelligences," including abstract, mechanical, and social. A few years later, psychologist David Wechsler recognized the importance of the noncognitive ("nonintellective") elements of intelligence, which he took to mean personal, affective, and social factors. He even proposed that these factors were essential for predicting a person's ability to succeed in life. In the late 1940s, the U.S. Office of Strategic Services (OSS) came up with an assessment that included communication, sensitivity, initiative, and interpersonal skills, which AT&T used in the 1950s.

Also in the 1950s, the Ohio State Leadership Studies suggested that effective leaders were able to establish "mutual trust, respect, and a certain warmth and rapport" with others in their group. Howard Gardner picked up on the preceding concepts when he wrote about "multiple intelligence" in the 1980s. In 1985, psychologist Reuven Bar-On recognized that people with high IQs didn't always succeed. He coined the term "emotional quotient" (EQ) and developed an instrument to measure what he also calls human effectiveness.

Emotional Intelligence

There was plenty of research going on, but it took the imagination of Peter Salovey at Yale University and John D. Mayer, now at the University of New Hampshire, to come up with the catchy term "emotional intelligence" in 1990. They also developed instruments to measure EI and help understand the practical implications of a high or low EI score in a person's life.

The way was paved for Daniel Goleman, a Harvard-trained psychologist and science writer for *The New York Times*, to bring the idea out of the research lab and into workplaces and the vernacular with the publication of his best-selling book, *Emotional Intelligence: Why It Can Matter More Than IQ* (Bantam).

Today, EI is a topic of research studies, books, consulting practices, and doctoral dissertations by the hundreds in fields from neuroscience to clinical psychology to education. Martin Seligman studies "learned optimism." In one study of freshmen at the University of Pennsylvania, he found that their scores on an optimism test were a better predictor of their freshman-year grades than their SAT scores or high school grades. Another study revealed one correlation between optimism and work: Optimistic insurance salesmen outsold their pessimistic counterparts by anywhere from 21 to 57 percent.

Other studies have shown that the ability to handle stress can predict net profits and sales per employee. One major financial services company discovered in the mid-1990s that the cause of low life insurance sales was emotional—a vicious cycle of negative emotions on the part of customers coupled with negative feelings on the part of the insurance advisers. When a group of advisers received twelve hours of emotional competence training, 90 percent of them increased their sales. Even the military has gotten in on the program. The U.S. Air Force used to dismiss up to 100 recruiters per year for failing to meet their quotas, losing as much as $3 million in training costs, as well as the missed quotas. In 1998, after administering EI tests to potential recruiters and hiring those who scored well on the test, turnover dropped to eight per year (*www.eiconsortium.com*). The Government Accountability Office subsequently asked all branches of the armed forces to adopt this procedure.

The Ten Habits of High EI People

High EI people share some behaviors and qualities. See how many of these describe you. High EI people:

1. Label feelings rather than people or situations
2. Distinguish between thoughts and feelings

3. Take responsibility for their feelings
4. Use their feelings to help them make decisions
5. Show respect for others' feelings
6. Feel energized, not angry
7. Validate other people's feelings
8. Practice getting a positive value from their negative emotions
9. Avoid commanding, controlling, judging, and lecturing others
10. Associate with other high EI people

Emotional Intelligence Test

For each item, rate from 1 to 5 how well you are able to display the ability described, with 1 being low ability and 5 being high ability. Try to think of real situations in which you have been called on to use each ability before you mark your score.

1.	Identify when you experience mood shifts	
2.	Regroup quickly after a setback	
3.	Act productively in situations that make you anxious	
4.	Know the impact that your behavior has on others	
5.	Communicate your feelings effectively	
6.	Associate different physical cues with different emotions	
7.	Relax when under pressure	
8.	Gear up at will	
9.	Develop consensus with others	
10.	Stay calm when you are the target of anger from others	
11.	Know when your self-talk is helpful	
12.	Calm yourself quickly when angry	

13.	Stop or change habits that aren't effective	
14.	Provide advice and support to others as needed	
15.	Accurately communicate what you experience	
16.	Know how you interpret events you encounter	
17.	Prioritize options when you are multitasking	
18.	Follow words with actions	
19.	Show empathy to others	
20.	Help a group manage emotions	
21.	Know when you are angry	
22.	Know when to step back from a situation	
23.	Develop new and more productive patterns of behavior	
24.	Recognize when others are distressed	
25.	Facilitate a discussion to solve a problem	

Scoring Your Test

Use the five domains, or competencies, of emotional intelligence to score your test. Mark your totals from the test for each item indicated.

Self-Awareness

These items indicate your ability to know what you are feeling at the moment; use that ability to guide your decision-making; realistically assess your own abilities; and promote a well-grounded sense of self-confidence.

1 _____

6 _____

11 _____   _____ **Your Self-Awareness Total**

16 _____

21 _____

Self-Regulation

These items indicate how well you handle your emotions so that they facilitate rather than interfere with the task at hand and how well you recover from emotional distress.

2 _____

7 _____

12 _____   _____ **Your Self-Regulation Total**

17 _____

22 _____

Self-Motivation

These items indicate how well you use emotional self-control to guide you toward your goals and how well you take initiative, strive to improve, and persevere in the face of setbacks and frustrations.

3 _____

8 _____

13 _____   _____ **Your Self-Motivation Total**

18 _____

23 _____

Empathy

These items indicate how well you sense what other people are feeling, your ability to take their perspective, and how well you cultivate rapport and attunement with a broad diversity of people.

4 _____

9 _____

14 _____   _____ **Your Empathy Total**

19 _____

24 _____

Social Understanding

These items indicate how effectively you handle emotions in relationships, how smoothly you interact with others, and how accurately you can read social situations in order to persuade, lead, negotiate, and settle disputes.

5 _____

10 _____

15 _____   _____ **Your Social Understanding Total**

20 _____

25 _____

Based on your response patterns, identify your two strongest emotional intelligence competencies and record them here and in the chart on page 179.

1. _____

2. _____

Now identify two EI competencies you want to improve and list them here and on the chart.

1. _____

2. _____

Now identify four specific tasks or strategies that will help you master these two emotional intelligence competencies (refer to the "Out with the Old, in with the New" section on page 172 for ideas).

1. _____

2. _____

3. _____

4. _____

*Jennifer Robinson, M.A., contributed to the development of this test.

Using Your Results

Correlating your score on this test with those from your values, skills, and interests tests should show you some patterns that you can use to further your career research. A person with a high EI score in empathy is likely to be drawn to careers in teaching, counseling, and other occupations involving social interaction, as opposed to careers that focus on clerical or administrative duties.

You can go about improving your EI the same way you would go about learning a sport, playing the piano, or driving a stick shift: practice. One psychologist likened improving EI as learning "a whole new language." With practice, you will grow comfortable with your self-awareness, self-regulation, self-motivation, empathy, and social understanding, and they will become second nature. Dr. Charles Spezzano has an elegant analogy in *What to Do Between Birth and Death: The Art of Growing Up* (Avon). He compares being adult (or for your purposes here, emotionally intelligent) to weight lifting. If you've been emotionally hurt, you get into the habit of "lifting as little emotional weight as possible" by avoiding or denying any emotion that causes you pain. It's easier, just as lifting light weights is easy. But lifting light weights doesn't build muscle, and avoiding emotions keeps you from growing and keeps you one step removed from life. He says the result is that you get "more and more out of shape emotionally."

If you're still not quite convinced about the value of EI, consider this: Emotional incompetence can be bad for your health. Sadness has been linked to low blood pressure, low energy, and lower immune responses; stress has been linked to immune responses, such as eczema; and out-of-control anger to heart attacks, strokes, headaches, and high blood pressure. One study at the Harvard School of Public Health followed 1,300 men over seven years. Those with the highest levels of anger were three times more likely to develop heart disease than the men with the lowest anger levels (*www.hotlib.com*).

Emotional Intelligence Matters

What can a high EI score do for you in the workplace? EI can do a lot more than you might think at first glance. Assuming your work requires you to interact with other people at least some of the time, EI can help you:

- Set, pursue, and achieve goals
- Work more efficiently
- Recruit and retain talent
- Get along with people
- Be sensitive to others' feelings
- Cope with difficult people
- Build customer loyalty
- Recognize lying
- Improve thinking
- Cope with unpleasant emotions
- Control your temper
- Work in and manage teams
- Grow more confident
- Head off arguments and resolve conflicts
- Rise to meet challenges

Emotional intelligence is an important thing, but it isn't the only thing. It can't guarantee you success any more than a high intelligence quotient will. But all things being equal—if you and your peers have similar academic credentials and intelligence—the scale tips in favor of the one with the higher EI.

Out with the Old, in with the New

Here are some tips to help you unlearn old habits and develop new ones as you work on your emotional competencies.

Self-Awareness

Find out more about you. The better you know yourself, the better you can recognize and manage your emotions. Spend some alone time in reflection. Try to identify the emotion you're feeling and how your body reacts to it. If it helps, write down your thoughts about your emotions. Choose your emotion. Decide to be more confident, happy, relaxed, or outgoing.

Pay attention to what triggers different emotional reactions in you. Try to think realistically about any given situation—and your reaction to it. If you're passed over for a promotion, rather than bemoaning your fate or cursing your boss, try to figure out why the other person was promoted. What skills does she exhibit that you may not have? Is she persuasive, empathetic, a good communicator? Does she collaborate well and foster trust? Once you figure that out, you can begin to improve those emotional competencies in yourself.

Self-Regulation

Practice delaying gratification and rewards.

Improve your coping skills. You don't have to react to everything immediately. Yes, write that irate e-mail, but don't send it.

Try to be less impulsive. If you get laid off, don't angrily burn your bridges; if someone seems to insult you in a meeting, don't snap at him or fire off a sniping e-mail later. Such actions can come back to haunt you—especially if there's the possibility of getting more work or a recommendation from your former employer or you've misinterpreted the situation with your coworker.

When your emotions get too heated, calm down. Count to ten, find the humor in the situation, meditate, and take a break. Time-outs work for unruly kids, and they can work for unruly emotions, too.

Break the cycle. For example, don't let irritation escalate into anger or sadness plummet into despondence. When you learn to recognize the signs such emotions cause in your body, you can calm down, analyze the situation, and start to fix it. If necessary, look into an anger management program.

Be proactive about finding solutions to problems rather than just fretting about them.

Teach yourself to replace negative or pessimistic thoughts with positive thoughts and actions.

Assert yourself and honor your needs. If you find yourself acquiescing to others or agreeing to help others to the detriment of your own needs, learn how to say a simple "no."

Remember your emotional budget. Don't squander your most earnest feelings on every little thing.

Self-Motivation

Realize how a well-developed emotional intelligence fits with your values and those goals and ideals most important to you.

Look back over the lists of values, skills, interests, and personality traits that you have compiled from the other tests in this book. You should be impressed with your unique qualities and inspired to find a career that incorporates them. Use this positive reinforcement to help you feel motivated to excel.

Work on a positive can-do attitude. The more confident you become in your abilities, the more likely you'll be able to stay motivated when you face challenges.

Set clear, specific, measurable, and realistic but challenging goals. If you have a big, long-range goal, break it up into smaller steps. You'll know what success feels like as you achieve each goal, and the task won't seem so overwhelming.

Give yourself deadlines so you know when you're making progress.

Find a motivational mentor, someone whose behaviors you admire and want to emulate. The person can be fictional, or even no longer alive, as long as he or she inspires you.

Give yourself a pep talk. You can be your own life coach. Pat yourself on the back when you do a good job and learn to give yourself positive feedback.

Visualize your success. Imagine yourself going through all the steps of the task you're avoiding, and then imagine how you feel when you've successfully completed it.

Empathy

Improve your listening skills. You may be hearing the words and think you know what the other person means, but also try restating what you're hearing to make sure you got it right. Make eye contact, nod, and refrain from interrupting.

Really try to understand where the other person is coming from. Try to think how you would feel in that situation. You know what they say: You don't really know your boss until you walk a mile in her shoes. It might not be as easy as you think.

Realize that it's easier to feel empathy for people you already agree with or who already do as you say. It's much harder to maintain that empathetic feeling if you're angry or frustrated. Remember that you can empathize with and disagree with someone at the same time.

Pay attention to body language and posture changes in other people as you talk to them and they talk to you.

Think of the words your boss or staff would use to describe you. How would you like them to describe you?

Do unto others as you would have them do unto you. It's a truism because it's true. If you're helpful and understanding toward your coworkers, they'll be more likely to act the same way toward you.

Focus on the positive rather than the negative. Don't just criticize a staff person's report because of its grammatical errors. Find something to compliment about it, too, such as the clear design or the quality of the writing.

Focus on others instead of yourself. We seem to live in a culture of entitlement where everyone "deserves" everything simply "because." Kindness requires empathy. Volunteer with an organization that helps people less fortunate than you. There's no better way to find out how lucky you really are.

Social Understanding

List the ways that improved EI could help you work with the people at your job.

Find ways to get people working together rather than at cross-purposes. Ask for help finding a solution to a problem, look for ways to compromise so everyone gets some part of what he wants, and give each person an equal turn to express her ideas or partake in a project.

Share. It's drilled into us as children, and it's just as important in the workplace. Learn to share tasks, resources, and, most especially, credit.

Build relationships based on trust. You need a few people you can express your emotions to honestly and openly.

Understand that other people's working or thinking styles can be different from yours. They aren't necessarily better or worse—just different. You can feed off another's drive to stay motivated or learn to ease up through another's more relaxed manner.

Express your appreciation of the work others are doing. No need to gush; keep it simple and sincere.

Learn good communication skills.

Give feedback in a way that encourages your staff to listen to you. If you ask for lots of ideas, don't then shoot them all down as "stupid." If you want staff to give feedback to you, don't fly off the handle if it's not all positive.

Remember that your posture, gestures, and facial expressions can express just as much (if not more) than your words can. Make sure they match your intent.

Chapter 12
Your Career Checkup

Congratulations! You have now completed some fairly rigorous self-assessment. You probably reaffirmed some personal preferences and eliminated some ideas that aren't for you. Along the way you no doubt learned a few things about yourself that you didn't know before. That's good! In this chapter, you'll put it all together into one chart that will help you plot your next steps. Noted psychologist Carl Jung once said, "Who looks outside, dreams; who looks inside, awakes." Get ready to awaken your true career potential.

Career Checkup Chart

As you have worked your way through the tests in this book, you have been recording your results on a photocopy of the following chart. If you haven't yet filled out the chart, do so now.

Values from Chapter 2		Value Type:	
Critical Values:	1. 2. 3. 4.	5 6. 7. 8.	
Critical values Missing from My situation:	1. 2.	3.	

Skills from Chapter 3		
Skill Category:		
Top Skills:		
Skill Category:		
Top Skills:		
Skills to Develop:		

Interests from Chapter 4		3-Letter RIASEC Code:	
Interest Area:	**Interest Area:**	**Interest Area:**	
Career Ideas:	*Career Ideas:*	*Career Ideas:*	

Personality from Chapter 5	
Personality Theme:	**Personality Theme:**
Traits:	*Traits:*

Work Environment from Chapter 6			
Priority Factors:	1. 2. 3. 4. 5.	6. 7. 8. 9. 10.	

Location from Chapter 7			
Requirements:	1. 2. 3. 4.	5. 6. 7. 8.	

Work/Life Balance from Chapter 8		**Score:**	
Goal Statements:			

Entrepreneurial Readiness from Chapter 9		**My Yes Total:**	
Comment:	**Ideas:**		

Managerial Suitability from Chapter 10		**Score:**	
Highest Scoring Areas:	**Areas for Growth:**		

Emotional Intelligence from Chapter 11	
Strongest Competencies: 1. 2.	**Areas for Improvement:** 1. 2.

What Your Chart Tells You

Now look at your completed chart. Do you see any patterns? What you see is a snapshot of you, your career aspirations, requirements, and potential. Remember back when you began this book looking for ideas on what to do about your stalled, boring, unsatisfactory, or nonexistent career? You've come quite a way since then.

What to Do Now?

You now have a blueprint for future action. Just as a doctor's checkup might indicate that you need to lose a few pounds, lower your blood pressure, and increase your stamina, your medical chart doesn't force you to do anything or necessarily tell you what to do to achieve those goals. But by knowing the results you want, you can develop a plan to eat more vegetables, cut back on salt, and add a walk to your daily routine. It's up to you now to come up with a plan to achieve your career goals.

Jot down any ideas that come to you in the spaces provided. The more specific and action-oriented they are, the more helpful they'll be to you in the long run. Don't worry. You don't have to do it all today.

Revisit Your Career-Change Options

This is the checklist from page 14. Look over the list again and see if your thoughts have changed. Would you still choose the same option that you picked when you began this book? Let your choice guide your actions as you implement the goals you recorded in the preceding chart. Ask a trusted friend, advisor, coach, or career counselor to help you brainstorm more options.

Depending on your current choice, there are many action steps you can try. **If you want to revitalize your current job:**

- Meet with your boss to renegotiate your current roles and responsibilities.
- Seek out classes or training programs to help you build new skills or enhance old ones.

- Find out if your company offers sabbaticals and if you qualify for one.
- Reconnect with an earlier passion through volunteer work.

If you want to make a work style change:

- Consider flextime.
- Explore telecommuting.
- Think about working part-time.
- Position yourself as a contractor or independent consultant.

If you want to make an internal move:

- Find ways to improve your managerial skills.
- Take workshops or specialized training.
- Identify an unfilled need in the organization and volunteer to do it.
- Let people know the types of projects in which you're interested.

If you want to make an external move:

- Look at other organizations where you might fit in.
- Identify different industries where your skills and expertise would be valued.
- Visit relocation Web sites and learn about other regions where you might want to live.
- Network with colleagues and members of your professional organizations.

If you want to make a complete career change:

- Go on informational interviews.
- Use published and online information available to you, such as those in the appendices.
- Determine if more education is needed.
- Learn how to repackage your skills and abilities.

If you're happy right where you are:

- Jot down five things you love about your job and look at the list periodically.
- Fraternize with your high-EI coworkers and let your mutual enthusiasm and optimism keep you energized.
- Set your own goals and rewards. It works for dieting, why not careers?
- Monitor your career satisfaction periodically so that you will know when it's time to make a change.

Informational Interviews

If you want still more information than you can find in publications or on the Internet, it's time to talk to people in the careers that interest you. If the field is new to you, the people in the trenches are the ones who can tell you what it's really like to work in those jobs on a daily basis. It may not be as glamorous as you think it is! But then, it might just be even more exciting and rewarding than you can even imagine.

If you've ever looked for work or held a job, you've no doubt had to endure one or a series of job interviews. They can be fun or excruciating, depending on your level of anxiety. Fortunately, informational interviews are a lot more enjoyable. After all, you just want to pick someone's brain about something about which they're passionate. Who wouldn't enjoy that? Here are some ways to make the most out of your informational interviewing experience.

Prepare Your Script

A script will help you to be prepared, just as you would be in a job interview. After all, you're asking to take up someone's valuable time. Don't leave them wondering why you bothered. Go ahead and jot down what you want to say. You don't want to read off a script, so memorize the salient points before the meeting.

- I am _____
- I have expertise in _____
- I'm interested in _____

Prepare Yourself

Remember that politeness counts! If in doubt, reread the chapter on emotional intelligence.

- Ask for twenty to thirty minutes of a person's time.
- Prepare your questions and your script ahead of time.
- Dress appropriately and arrive on time.
- Stick to the allotted time.
- Write a prompt thank you.
- Send any agreed-upon follow-up material.
- Let each person know what you decide in the future.

Ask the Right Questions

Depending on the career, what you already know about it, your level of familiarity with the person you're interviewing, and a host of other factors, your questions will vary from these. Here are a few to get you thinking.

- Could you give me a brief overview of your role and responsibilities?
- What do you do on a typical day?
- Did you receive any formal or informal company training?
- What are the major rewards and frustrations of your job?
- What skills do you use the most?
- What have been some of your most interesting or difficult challenges?
- How did you make your transition?
- What associations or publications are relevant to this field?
- What personal qualities are important for this position or industry?
- What is the best piece of career advice you have ever been given?

- What kind of opportunities does this field hold for someone with my skills and experience?
- What is the salary range for someone with my expertise?
- If I were interested in a position or career such as yours, what steps would you recommend I take?
- Where do you think the opportunities will be within _____ (months/years) in the future?
- Can you recommend other people with whom I should talk?
- When I get more focused, may I call you again?

Prepare to Take Action!

You've put in a good deal of hard work and gotten this far, but perhaps there is still something holding you back from attaining your ideal career. What's stopping you? That's not always easy to figure out, but it can be helpful to try to identify some of the things that are keeping you from career fulfillment. Look at the following list and check any that apply to you.

- ❑ Lack of confidence
- ❑ Reluctance to take risks
- ❑ Health
- ❑ Assumed discrimination
- ❑ Lack of occupational information
- ❑ Lack of role models
- ❑ Difficulty following through
- ❑ Money pressures
- ❑ Time constraints
- ❑ Family constraints
- ❑ Unrealistic goals

Doing more research into various careers and what they entail can help you with some of the preceding concerns. Also, don't forget that there are professional career counselors and coaches who are trained to help you attain your goal. Just like any good coach of a sports team, they can offer encouragement, support, and a healthy reality check. They also have a wealth of information—resources, ideas, and people to contact that you may not have thought of or even known about. Think of them like that friendly person in the visitor center you meet on vacation. Map in hand, you know you want to get from point A to point B, but she knows where to find the best restaurants and schools, parks, shops, and those unique spots that make a trip memorable. You have your career map; all you may need now is a little guidance.

If there's nothing stopping you from going ahead, take the time to jot down some concrete action steps that you can do right now and some that you can do in the future.

Action Steps (short-term):

_____

_____

_____

_____

_____

Action Steps (long-term):

_____

_____

_____

_____

_____

As Nick Paumgarten wrote in *The New Yorker* (April 2006), "a map contains multitudes." That's true whether you're driving from Secaucus to Phoenix or plotting the course of your career. There are infinite things to see and do on the journey, many ways to get sidetracked and lost, and great surprises to be enjoyed along the way. Preparation will make sure you don't run out of sustenance or energy. A good map will keep you on the right track. The rest of the adventure is up to you.

Appendix A

Published and Online Career Resources

There should be something helpful to you in the following general resources no matter what tweak, change, or overhaul you have in mind for your career. There are lots more out there, too. Check your local library and do some Web searches to find exactly the right information for your situation.

General Career and Job-Hunting Resources

Bolles, Richard N. *What Color Is Your Parachute?* Berkeley, CA: Ten Speed Press, 2006.

Eikleberry, Carol, Ph.D. *The Career Guide for Creative and Unconventional People.* Berkeley, CA: Ten Speed Press, 1995.

U.S. Department of Labor. *Occupational Outlook Handbook* (revised and updated every two years).

These online sites are useful for general career information as well as job-hunting tips and ideas.

AllBusiness
www.allbusiness.com
Information and forms for small businesses

BestJobsUSA
www.bestjobsusa.com
General purpose employment site operated by Recourse Communications, Inc.

Bizjournals
www.bizjournals.com
Links to Web sites of over forty print business journals

CareerBuilder.com
www.careerbuilder.com

Career Explorer
www.careerexplorer.net

CareerJournal.com
www.careerjournal.com
General purpose employment site from *The Wall Street Journal*

The Career Key
www.careerkey.org

Career advice, planning, and resources

Career Momentum, Inc.
www.careermomentum.com
Career advice, clinics, and information

CareerOneStop
www.careeronestop.org
Site sponsored by the U.S. Department of Labor that includes America's Career InfoNet (*www.CareerInfoNet.org*) which includes national, state, and local career information and labor market data; America's Job Bank (*www.ajb.org*), the nation's largest labor exchange; America's Service Locator (*www.ServiceLocator.org*) with information about workforce centers, unemployment benefits, job training, education, and other services.

Careers.org
www.careers.org
Job, career, and education information and links

Challenger, Gray & Christmas, Inc.

www.challengergray.com

Outplacement firm for executives, middle managers, and long-term employees; Web site includes press releases with current job-related news.

CNN Money

http://money.cnn.com

The Internet home of the publications *Fortune, Money, Business 2.0,* and *Fortune Small Business*

Computerwork.com

www.computerwork.com

Specialty employment site focusing on information technology professionals

Craigslist

www.craigslist.com

A community site that also has job listings in many cities around the world

Dice

www.dice.com

Specialty employment site focusing on information technology and engineering professionals

eFinancialCareers.com

www.efinancialcareers.com

Site that focuses on jobs in banking and financial sector

EmploymentGuide.com

www.employmentguide.com

General-purpose employment site affiliated with the print *Employment Guide* distributed outside convenience stores in the United States

ExecuNet

www.execunet.com

Specialty employment site focusing on executives earning $100,000 per year or more

FabJob

www.fabjob.com

Information for finding your "dream career"

Fast Company

www.fastcompany.com

Management, leadership, and career advice for business executives

Futurestep

www.futurestep.com

Middle management recruitment

HealtheCareers Network

www.healthecareers.com

Specialty employment portal connecting to over sixty medical and health care-related associations

HealtheHire

www.healthehire.com

Information and job-posting Web site for health-care professionals

HRJobs.com

www.hrjobs.com

An association-based employment site that specializes in human resource management professionals

Idealist.org

www.idealist.org

Nonprofit job listings by region.

InformationWeek

✍www.informationweek.com

"Business innovation powered by technology"

JobCentral

✍www.jobcentral.com

Job board and employment Web site for nation-wide employment opportunities.

Job-hunt.org

✍www.jobhunt.org

Job search guide and career resource center

JobsInLogistics

✍www.jobsinlogistics.com

Specialty employment site that focuses on transportation, supply chain, and other logistics professionals

JobsintheMoney

✍www.jobsinthemoney.com

Specialty job site for accounting and finance professionals

Jobs.net

✍www.jobs.net

Job hunting by location or category, as well as job-hunting tips and information

LatPro.com

✍www.latpro.com

Employment site that focuses on Hispanic and bilingual professionals

LiveCareer

✍www.livecareer.com

Free online career interest test

MarketingJobs.com

✍www.marketingjobs.com

Specialty employment site focusing on sales, marketing, and advertising jobs

Mediabistro.com

✍www.mediabistro.com

Specialty Web site for people working with media content

Monster.com

✍www.monster.com

Job-hunting help and career advice

MRINetwork.com

✍www.mrinetwork.com

Business recruitment firm

NationJob.com

✍www.nationjob.com

Job search, career, employment, and resume services for job seekers

Net-Temps

✍www.net-temps.com

Site that serves the staffing industry in both direct placement and temporary hiring

6FigureJobs

✍www.6figurejobs.com

Site that focuses on $100,000 per year executives and openings

TalentZoo.com

www.talentzoo.com

Specialty employment site that focuses on the advertising, marketing, and public relations industries and latest industry news

TopUSAJobs.com

www.topusajobs.com

General-purpose employment site

TrueCareers

www.truecareers.com

Site owned by student loan company Sallie Mae focuses on jobs for degreed professionals

USAJobs

www.usajobs.com

The U.S. government's official job site

Vault

www.vault.com

General purpose employment site that also publishes books and other resources for job seekers and employers

VetJobs.com

www.vetjobs.com

Specialty site that focuses on employment for U.S. military veterans and their families

Winning Workplaces

www.winningworkplaces.org

"Promoting workplace culture that makes dollars and sense"

Work Ministry

www.workministry.com

Job-support groups sponsored by faith-based and community organizations

Workopolis

www.workopolis.com

A Canada-based general purpose employment site owned by Bell Globemedia, Toronto Star Newspapers, and Gesca, Ltd.

WorkTree.com

www.worktree.com

Job-search portal

Yahoo! HotJobs

http://hotjobs.yahoo.com

General purpose employment site affiliated with the Internet portal Yahoo!

ZoomInfo

www.zoominfo.com

A search engine that focuses on information on individuals

Values

Henderson, Michael. *Finding True North*. Aukland, NZ: HarperCollins, 2003.

Rokeach, Milton. *The Nature of Human Values*. New York: Free Press, 1973.

Rokeach, Milton. *Understanding Human Values: Individual and Societal*. New York: Free Press, 1979.

Seligman, Martin E. P. *Authentic Happiness*. New York: Free Press, 2002.

Minessence Group

www.minessence.net

An Australian organization that has created its own values inventory (AVI). There are many articles and documents about values on this Web site.

Positive Psychology Center

www.ppc.sas.upenn.edu

Promotes research, training, education, dissemination, and the application of positive psychology

Skills

Achieve, Inc.

www.achieve.org

Created by the nation's governors and business leaders in 1996, Achieve helps states raise academic standards and achievement so that all students graduate ready for college, work, and citizenship.

Information and Communication Technologies (ITC) Literacy

www.ictliteracy.info

The ICT Literacy Portal is focused on promoting information and communication technologies (ICT) digital literacy. The Web site provides a global resource and collaborative environment for dissemination of ICT literacy materials, interactive discussions, research information, and international dialogue.

National Association of Colleges and Employers

www.naceweb.org

Professional association offering information on the employment of the college educated, con-

necting more than 5,200 college career services professionals at nearly 2,000 college and universities nationwide

National Consortium on Health Science and Technology Education

www.nchste.org

A national partnership of individuals and organizations with a vested interest in health science and technology education organized in 1991 to stimulate creative and innovative leadership for ensuring a well-prepared health care workforce

U.S. Department of Labor Bureau of Labor Statistics

www.bls.gov/ept

Information on employer-provided training

U.S. Department of Labor Employment and Training Administration

http://online.onetcenter.org/skills

Occupational Information network that offers lots of detail about job-related skills

Interests

Holland, John. *The Psychology of Vocational Choice*. Waltham, MA: Blaisdell, 1966.

U.S. Department of Labor Employment and Training Administration

http://online.onetcenter.org

Lots of information about occupations

Personality

Baron, Renee. *What Type Am I? Discover Who You Really Are*. New York: Penguin Books, 1998.

Espeland, Pamela. *Knowing Me, Knowing You: The I-Sight Way to Understand Yourself and Others*. Minneapolis, MN: Free Spirit, 2001.

Keirsey, David. *Please Understand Me II: Temperament Character Intelligence*. Prometheus Nemesis Book Co., 1998.

Kroeger, Otto, and Janet M. Thuesen. *Type Talk: The 16 Personality Types That Determine How We Live, Love, and Work*. New York: Dell Publishing, 1988.

Tieger, Paul D., and Barbara Barron-Tieger. *Do What You Are*. New York: Little, Brown & Co., 2001.

American Psychological Association
www.apa.org
Psychology research, news, and more

Dr. C. George Boeree, Psychology Department, Shippensburg University
www.ship.edu
Good overviews on the various personality theories and the major players, as well as some links to other sources

CPP, Inc.
www.cpp.com
Publisher and provider of products and services for professionals focused on meeting individual and organizational development needs; publishes and administers the MBTI and other instruments

The Enneagram
www.ennea.com
Web site devoted to the Enneagram offering information, books, and other resources.

Keirsey.com
www.keirsey.com
David Keirsey's Web site explains the Keirsey Temperament Sorter and offers his publications for sale.

The Myers & Briggs Foundation
www.myersbriggs.org
Books and other information about the Myers-Briggs Type Indicator

9Types.com
www.9types.com
Information on the Enneagram

The Personality Project
www.personality-project.org
General and academic information and links to personality research

Work Environment

Bixler, Susan, and Nancy Nix-Rice. *The New Professional Image*. Avon, MA: Adams Media, 2005.

Advanced Brain Technologies

www.advancedbrain.com

Develops innovative brain training products to human potential

American Telecommuting Association

www.yourATA.com

Information on telecommuting and policies for employers

Architecture Week

www.architectureweek.com

Magazine that includes articles on green, livable, and sustainable design and building

The Business Research Lab

www.busreslab.com

Employee and business surveys and information

Cornell University Ergonomics Web

http://ergo.human.cornell.edu

Information from research studies and class work by students and faculty in the Cornell Human Factors and Ergonomics Research Group (CHFERG)

The Ergonomics Society

www.ergonomics.org.uk

This U.K.-based society has links and all kinds of information about ergonomics.

ITAC (International Telework Association and Council)

www.workingfromanywhere.org

A nonprofit organization dedicated to advancing the growth and success of work independent of location; Web site includes news and resources.

theOffice™

www.theofficeonline.com

Web site for this paid work space for writers and others who need an office environment away from home and office

Office Ergonomics Training

http://office-ergo.com

Research and tips on office ergonomics, including things to look for that can cause problems in office setting, as well as possible solutions

The Telework Coalition

www.telcoa.org

Nonprofit that advocates telecommuting and telework

UCLA Ergonomics

www.ergonomics.ucla.edu

Practical information about ergonomics

U.S. Department of Labor Occupational Safety & Health Administration

www.osha.gov

Information about ergonomics and the various health effects caused by office equipment that isn't ergonomically designed

U.S. Equal Employment Opportunity Commission

www.eeoc.gov

Government Web site with information about workplace discrimination, laws, regulations, and current news

Winning Workplaces

www.winningworkplaces.org

Group devoted to helping organizations create great workplaces; provides small and midsize employers with proven, practical, and affordable consulting, training, and information on strategies to improve workplace practices; Web site includes resources, research studies, and more.

Location

If you're contemplating a move to another city, be sure to check the Web site of that city's Chamber of Commerce, as well as a few issues of the local newspapers and their Web sites.

Calthorpe, Peter. *The Next American Metropolis.* Princeton Arch, 1995.

The City Repair Project

www.cityrepair.org

An all-volunteer grassroots organization that helps people reclaim urban spaces to create community-oriented places

Find Your Spot

www.findyourspot.com

Take their online quiz and get a tailored list of the best cities and small towns that fit your criteria.

Homefair.com

www.homefair.com

Relocation information

Housing Leaders

www.housingleaders.com

Source for information about real estate, new houses, rentals, agents, brokers, foreclosures, and mortgages

Morgan Quitno Press

www.morganquitno.com

Private research and publishing company that specializes in reference books that compare states and cities in several different subject areas; publications include State Rankings, Health Care State Rankings, Crime State Rankings, Education State Rankings, State Trends, and City Crime Rankings. The company also annually publishes 350 other state-specific publications, good sources of comparative and objective statistics.

Partners for Livable Communities

www.mostlivable.org

America's Most Livable Communities is a project of Partners for Livable Communities, a national nonprofit working to restore and renew U.S. communities. Partners has long been champion of the economics of amenities: the interrelationship between a community's quality of life and its ability to attract and retain business investments, stimulate convention and visitor trade, increase downtown retail activity, and improve the city's image to residents and nonresidents alike.

Population Reference Bureau

www.prb.org

The Population Reference Bureau informs people around the world about population, health, and the environment and empowers them to use that information to advance the well-being of current and future generations.

Sperling's BestPlaces

www.bestplaces.net

Demographics, preferences, and information about the best places to live, work, or retire

U.S. Census Bureau

www.census.gov

Lots of information about people and households in the United States

Work/Life Balance

Putnam, Robert D. *Bowling Alone: The Collapse and Revival of American Community.* New York: Simon & Schuster, 2000.

Welch, Jack, and Suzy Welch. *Winning.* New York: HarperCollins, 2005.

The Alfred P. Sloan Foundation

www.sloan.org

Information about the foundation's Workplace, Workforce and Working Families program

Alliance for Work-Life Progress (AWLP)

www.awlp.org

This membership organization is committed to the development and advancement of the field of work-life effectiveness, addressing work-life issues through publications, forums, and professional development strategies. AWLP strives to improve the professionalism of those working in

the work-life arena and to influence better integration of work and family life.

Families and Work Institute

www.familiesandwork.org

A nonprofit center for research that provides data to inform decision-making on the changing workforce, changing family, and changing community

Women Entrepreneurs Inc.

www.we-inc.org

Organization devoted to helping women entrepreneurs through networking, educational programs, and advocacy

Workforce Management

www.workforce.com

Information on workplace law, training and development, management, benefits, and other human resources topics

Entrepreneurship

Canada, C. K. *13 Small Businesses You Can Start on a Shoestring Budget.* e-book

Pink, Daniel. *Free Agent Nation: The Future of Working for Yourself.* Warner Business Books, 2002.

Urquhart-Brown, Susan. *The Accidental Entrepreneur: Practical Wisdom for People Who Never Expected to Work for Themselves.* Oakland, CA: Career Steps, 2004.

Belmont University Center for Entrepreneurship

www.belmont.edu

The Daring Micropreneur Show

✍*www.smallbizgames.com/sbgdm.htm*
Interviews and practical advice from home and small business owners for small business owners, home business owners, entrepreneurs, and start-ups

Entrepreneur Magazine

✍*www.entrepreneur.com*

Leading Women Entrepreneurs of the World

✍*www.leadingwomen.org*
A nonprofit organization established to identify, honor, promote, and encourage female entrepreneurial excellence

The Library of Economics and Liberty

✍*www.econlib.org*
The Concise Encyclopedia of Economics

National Association for the Self-Employed

✍*www.nase.org*

U.S. Department of Labor Web Site for Women Entrepreneurs

✍*www.women-21.gov*
Web site created by the Department of Labor and the Small Business Administration for women entrepreneurs

Women Entrepreneurs Inc.

✍*www.we-inc.org*
Organization founded to help women entrepreneurs succeed through networking, educational programs, and advocacy

Managerial Suitability

Bacharach, Samuel B. *Keep Them on Your Side: Leading and Managing for Momentum.* Avon, MA: Adams Media, 2006.

Blanchard, Kenneth H., and Spencer Johnson. *One Minute Manager.* Partnership and Candle Business Communications Corporation, 1982.
Boylan, Bob. *Get Everyone in Your Boat Rowing in the Same Direction.* Avon, MA: Adams Media, 1993.

Buckingham, Marcus, and Curt Coffman. *First, Break All the Rules: What the World's Greatest Managers Do Differently.* New York: Simon & Schuster, 1999.

Collins, Jim. *Good to Great: Why Some Companies Make the Leap and Others Don't.* New York: HarperCollins, 2001.

Deci, Edward, Ph.D. *Why We Do What We Do: Understanding Self-Motivation.* New York: Penguin, 1995.

Payne, John, and Shirley Payne. *Management Basics.* Avon, MA: Adams Media, 1998.

Pincus, Marilyn. *Managing Difficult People: A Survival Guide for Handling Any Employee.* Avon, MA: Adams Media, 2004.

Rath, Tom, and Donald O. Clifton. *How Full Is Your Bucket? Positive Strategies for Work and Life.* New York: Gallup Press, 2004.

Yate, Martin, and Peter Sander. *Knock 'em Dead Management.* Avon, MA: Adams Media, 2005.

American Management Association

🖋*www.amanet.org*

Nonprofit, membership-based association that provides management development and educational services to individuals, companies, and government agencies worldwide

Dr. Robert Brooks

🖋*www.drrobertbrooks.com*

A clinical psychologist at Harvard Medical School who speaks on the themes of resilience, self-esteem, motivation, and family relationships, his Web site features monthly articles on these topics.

The Gallup Poll

🖋*www.gallup.com*

National Resource Center

🖋*www.ccfbest.org*

"Best of the Best" e-newsletter with articles on communications, partnerships, and more

Emotional Intelligence

Andrews, Linda Wasmer. *Intelligence*. Danbury, CT: Franklin Watts, 2003.

Bar-On, Reuven, and James D. A. Parker, eds., *Handbook of Emotional Intelligence*. San Francisco, CA: Jossey-Bass, 1999.

Cherniss, Cary, and Daniel Goleman, eds. *The Emotionally Intelligent Workplace*. San Francisco, CA: Jossey-Bass, 2001.

Druskat, Vanessa Urch, Ph.D., Fabio Sala, Ph.D., and Gerald Mount, Ph.D., eds., *Linking Emotional Intelligence and Performance at Work*. EI Consortium, 2006.

Goleman, Daniel. *Emotional Intelligence: Why It Can Matter More than IQ*. New York: Bantam Books, 1995.

Goleman, Daniel. *Working with Emotional Intelligence*. New York: Bantam Books, 1998.

Gonzales-Molina, Gabriel, and Durt Coffman. *Follow This Path: How the World's Greatest Organizations Drive Growth by Unleashing Human Potential*. Warner Books, 2002.

Pink, Daniel H. *A Whole New Mind*. New York: Riverhead Books, 2005.

Riggio, Ronald E., and Robert S. Feldman, eds. *Applications of Nonverbal Communication*. Mahwah, NJ: Lawrence Erlbaum Associates, 2005.

Spezzano, Charles, Ph.D. *What to Do Between Birth and Death: The Art of Growing Up*. Avon Books, 1992.

Stein, Steven J., Ph.D., and Howard E. Book, M.D. *The EQ Edge*. Multi-Health Systems, 2001.

AAA Foundation for Traffic Safety

🖋*www.aaafoundation.org*

Information on road rage and aggressive driving

Center for Creative Leadership

✎www.ccl.org

Consortium for Research on Emotional Intelligence in Organizations

✎www.eiconsortium.org

Its mission is to aid the advancement of research and practice related to emotional intelligence in organizations.

Institute for Organizational Performance

✎www.eqperformance.com

Six Seconds is a nonprofit organization founded to bring emotional intelligence into practice in organizations, schools, and communities. It creates emotional intelligence learning and development tools. The Institute for Organizational Performance was created to bring this learning technology to the organizational market.

University of New Hampshire

✎www.unh.edu/emotional_intelligence

Emotional Intelligence Information is a site maintained by John D. Mayer and others dedicated to communicating scientific information about emotional intelligence, including relevant aspects of emotions, cognition, and personality

Wharton School, University of Pennsylvania

✎http://knowledge.wharton.upenn.edu

Information on leadership, emotional intelligence, and other issues relating to management and business

Appendix B

Career Counseling Services and Other Instruments

Check your local telephone directory, do Web searches, and ask colleagues for recommendations if you're searching for a career professional. Also, the career counseling departments of many colleges and universities offer online information and tests. Lots of relocation businesses and services have long or short quizzes on their Web sites that will help you find a place in the country—or the world—that suits you.

Remember that many popular career instruments, such as the Myers-Briggs Type Indicator (MBTI), Strong Interest Inventory (SII), and Campbell Skills and Interests Inventory (CSII) can only be administered by people who have completed a qualifying program and can help you interpret your results.

Bay Area Career Center

57 Post Street, Suite 804
San Francisco, CA 94104
(415) 398-4881
✎www.bayareacareercenter.com
Credentialed career counselors and coaches, relevant workshops, job support groups, and an Informational Interview Network help you find your direction and make successful changes in your work life.

Discovery Your Personality

✎www.discoveryourpersonality.com
MBTI tests online and phone consultations

Elevations, the Career Discovery Tool

✎www.ElevateYourCareer.com
Career assessment, evaluation, networking, coaching, and more information about the Elevations tests excerpted in this book

Emotional Intelligence

✎www.emotionaliq.com
MSCEIT test measuring emotional intelligence and certification for administering test

EQ University

✎www.equniversity.com
Emotional intelligence assessment, training, and development

Mark Guterman, M.A., Career Consultant

✎www.meaningfulcareers.com
Mark@.meaningfulcareers.com
Counseling, books, articles, and other resources for guiding your career

Holland Types

✎ http://facweb.bhc.edu/advising/counseling/
services/develop/interests.htm#holland's
Information about Holland Types on Web site of Black Hawk College

Robin B. Holt, M.A., Career Consultant

rholt@bayareacareercenter.com

Humanetrics.com

✎www.humanmetrics.com
Jung Topology test and other personality tests

International Personality Item Pool (IPIP)

✎www.personal.psu.edu/faculty/j/5/j5j/IPIP/
Take the original 300-item IPIP or a shorter version to estimate where you stand on five personality domains and thirty subdomains

Internet Career Connection

✎www.iccweb.com
Online interest inventory

Janda, Louis, *Ph.D. Career Tests.* Avon, MA: Adams Media, 1999.
Twenty-five tests covering many aspects of the career decision process

JobHuntersBible.com
✐*www.jobhuntersbible.com*
Web site of Richard Bolles, author of *What Color Is Your Parachute?* Berkeley, CA: Ten Speed Press, 2006.

Terry Karp, M.A., Career Consultant
tkarp@bayareacareercenter.com

Keirsey.com
✐*www.keirsey.com*
Keirsey Temperament Sorter, descriptions of the various temperaments, and some famous people in each category

LiveCareer
✐*www.livecareer.com*
Free online career interest test

Mind Garden, Inc.
✐*www.mindgarden.com*
Publisher of psychological assessments and instruments

O-Net Resource Center
✐*www.onetcenter.org*
Interest profiler and other career exploration instruments on Web site run by the U.S. Department of Labor

The Personality Page
✐*www.personalitypage.com*
Personality tests and information

Personality Test Center
✐*www.personalitytest.net*
Personality tests

PersonalityType.com
✐*www.personalitytype.com*
Personality quiz by Paul D. Tieger and Barbara Barron-Tieger, authors of *Do What You Are*

QueenDom.com
✐*www.queendom.com*
Large Web site with free and fee-based self-assessment tests in the fields of careers, personality, psychology, relationships, intelligence, and health; also offering advice, community, surveys, and trivia quizzes on many subjects

Helen M. Scully, M.A., Career Consultant
✐*www.ScullyCareerAssociates.com*

SimilarMinds.com
✐*http://similarminds.com/personality_tests.html*
Variety of personality tests

Dena Sneider, M.A., Career Consultant
dsneider@bayareacareercenter.com

Tickle
✐*www.tickle.com*
Personality, relationship, and other online tests

TypeFocus Careers

✍*www.typefocus.com*
Personality assessment and career counseling

Susan Urquhart-Brown, M.A., Career Consultant and Business Coach

susanub@careersteps123.com
Help for fledgling business owners who want to
build successful, thriving businesses
✍*www.careersteps123.com*

Yahoo! Geocities Personality Tests

✍*www.geocities.com/lifexplore/tests.htm*
Links to lots of different personality tests

Index

THE EVERYTHING SERIES!

BUSINESS & PERSONAL FINANCE

Everything® Accounting Book
Everything® Budgeting Book
Everything® Business Planning Book
Everything® Coaching and Mentoring Book
Everything® Fundraising Book
Everything® Get Out of Debt Book
Everything® Grant Writing Book
Everything® Home-Based Business Book, 2nd Ed.
Everything® Homebuying Book, 2nd Ed.
Everything® Homeselling Book, 2nd Ed.
Everything® Investing Book, 2nd Ed.
Everything® Landlording Book
Everything® Leadership Book
Everything® Managing People Book, 2nd Ed.
Everything® Negotiating Book
Everything® Online Auctions Book
Everything® Online Business Book
Everything® Personal Finance Book
Everything® Personal Finance in Your 20s and 30s Book
Everything® Project Management Book
Everything® Real Estate Investing Book
Everything® Robert's Rules Book, $7.95
Everything® Selling Book
Everything® Start Your Own Business Book, 2nd Ed.
Everything® Wills & Estate Planning Book

COOKING

Everything® Barbecue Cookbook
Everything® Bartender's Book, $9.95
Everything® Chinese Cookbook
Everything® Classic Recipes Book
Everything® Cocktail Parties and Drinks Book
Everything® College Cookbook
Everything® Cooking for Baby and Toddler Book
Everything® Cooking for Two Cookbook
Everything® Diabetes Cookbook
Everything® Easy Gourmet Cookbook
Everything® Fondue Cookbook
Everything® Fondue Party Book
Everything® Gluten-Free Cookbook
Everything® Glycemic Index Cookbook
Everything® Grilling Cookbook

Everything® Healthy Meals in Minutes Cookbook
Everything® Holiday Cookbook
Everything® Indian Cookbook
Everything® Italian Cookbook
Everything® Low-Carb Cookbook
Everything® Low-Fat High-Flavor Cookbook
Everything® Low-Salt Cookbook
Everything® Meals for a Month Cookbook
Everything® Mediterranean Cookbook
Everything® Mexican Cookbook
Everything® One-Pot Cookbook
Everything® Quick and Easy 30-Minute, 5-Ingredient Cookbook
Everything® Quick Meals Cookbook
Everything® Slow Cooker Cookbook
Everything® Slow Cooking for a Crowd Cookbook
Everything® Soup Cookbook
Everything® Tex-Mex Cookbook
Everything® Thai Cookbook
Everything® Vegetarian Cookbook
Everything® Wild Game Cookbook
Everything® Wine Book, 2nd Ed.

GAMES

Everything® 15-Minute Sudoku Book, $9.95
Everything® 30-Minute Sudoku Book, $9.95
Everything® Blackjack Strategy Book
Everything® Brain Strain Book, $9.95
Everything® Bridge Book
Everything® Card Games Book
Everything® Card Tricks Book, $9.95
Everything® Casino Gambling Book, 2nd Ed.
Everything® Chess Basics Book
Everything® Craps Strategy Book
Everything® Crossword and Puzzle Book
Everything® Crossword Challenge Book
Everything® Cryptograms Book, $9.95
Everything® Easy Crosswords Book
Everything® Easy Kakuro Book, $9.95
Everything® Games Book, 2nd Ed.
Everything® Giant Sudoku Book, $9.95
Everything® Kakuro Challenge Book, $9.95
Everything® Large-Print Crossword Challenge Book
Everything® Large-Print Crosswords Book
Everything® Lateral Thinking Puzzles Book, $9.95
Everything® Mazes Book

Everything® Pencil Puzzles Book, $9.95
Everything® Poker Strategy Book
Everything® Pool & Billiards Book
Everything® Test Your IQ Book, $9.95
Everything® Texas Hold 'Em Book, $9.95
Everything® Travel Crosswords Book, $9.95
Everything® Word Games Challenge Book
Everything® Word Search Book

HEALTH

Everything® Alzheimer's Book
Everything® Diabetes Book
Everything® Health Guide to Adult Bipolar Disorder
Everything® Health Guide to Controlling Anxiety
Everything® Health Guide to Fibromyalgia
Everything® Health Guide to Thyroid Disease
Everything® Hypnosis Book
Everything® Low Cholesterol Book
Everything® Massage Book
Everything® Menopause Book
Everything® Nutrition Book
Everything® Reflexology Book
Everything® Stress Management Book

HISTORY

Everything® American Government Book
Everything® American History Book
Everything® Civil War Book
Everything® Freemasons Book
Everything® Irish History & Heritage Book
Everything® Middle East Book

HOBBIES

Everything® Candlemaking Book
Everything® Cartooning Book
Everything® Coin Collecting Book
Everything® Drawing Book
Everything® Family Tree Book, 2nd Ed.
Everything® Knitting Book
Everything® Knots Book
Everything® Photography Book
Everything® Quilting Book
Everything® Scrapbooking Book
Everything® Sewing Book
Everything® Woodworking Book

HOME IMPROVEMENT

Bolded titles are new additions to the series.
All Everything® books are priced at $12.95 or $14.95, unless otherwise stated. Prices subject to change without notice.

Everything® Feng Shui Book
Everything® Feng Shui Decluttering Book, $9.95
Everything® Fix-It Book
Everything® Home Decorating Book
Everything® Home Storage Solutions Book
Everything® Homebuilding Book
Everything® Lawn Care Book
Everything® Organize Your Home Book

KIDS' BOOKS

All titles are $7.95

Everything® Kids' Animal Puzzle & Activity Book
Everything® Kids' Baseball Book, 4th Ed.
Everything® Kids' Bible Trivia Book
Everything® Kids' Bugs Book
Everything® Kids' Cars and Trucks Puzzle & Activity Book
Everything® Kids' Christmas Puzzle & Activity Book
Everything® Kids' Cookbook
Everything® Kids' Crazy Puzzles Book
Everything® Kids' Dinosaurs Book
Everything® Kids' First Spanish Puzzle and Activity Book
Everything® Kids' Gross Hidden Pictures Book
Everything® Kids' Gross Jokes Book
Everything® Kids' Gross Mazes Book
Everything® Kids' Gross Puzzle and Activity Book
Everything® Kids' Halloween Puzzle & Activity Book
Everything® Kids' Hidden Pictures Book
Everything® Kids' Horses Book
Everything® Kids' Joke Book
Everything® Kids' Knock Knock Book
Everything® Kids' Learning Spanish Book
Everything® Kids' Math Puzzles Book
Everything® Kids' Mazes Book
Everything® Kids' Money Book
Everything® Kids' Nature Book
Everything® Kids' Pirates Puzzle and Activity Book
Everything® Kids' Princess Puzzle and Activity Book
Everything® Kids' Puzzle Book
Everything® Kids' Riddles & Brain Teasers Book
Everything® Kids' Science Experiments Book
Everything® Kids' Sharks Book
Everything® Kids' Soccer Book
Everything® Kids' Travel Activity Book

KIDS' STORY BOOKS

Everything® Fairy Tales Book

LANGUAGE

Everything® Conversational Chinese Book with

CD, $19.95
Everything® Conversational Japanese Book with CD, $19.95
Everything® French Grammar Book
Everything® French Phrase Book, $9.95
Everything® French Verb Book, $9.95
Everything® German Practice Book with CD, $19.95
Everything® Inglés Book
Everything® Learning French Book
Everything® Learning German Book
Everything® Learning Italian Book
Everything® Learning Latin Book
Everything® Learning Spanish Book
Everything® Russian Practice Book with CD, $19.95
Everything® Sign Language Book
Everything® Spanish Grammar Book
Everything® Spanish Phrase Book, $9.95
Everything® Spanish Practice Book with CD, $19.95
Everything® Spanish Verb Book, $9.95

MUSIC

Everything® Drums Book with CD, $19.95
Everything® Guitar Book
Everything® Guitar Chords Book with CD, $19.95
Everything® Home Recording Book
Everything® Music Theory Book with CD, $19.95
Everything® Reading Music Book with CD, $19.95
Everything® Rock & Blues Guitar Book (with CD), $19.95
Everything® Songwriting Book

NEW AGE

Everything® Astrology Book, 2nd Ed.
Everything® Birthday Personology Book
Everything® Dreams Book, 2nd Ed.
Everything® Love Signs Book, $9.95
Everything® Numerology Book
Everything® Paganism Book
Everything® Palmistry Book
Everything® Psychic Book
Everything® Reiki Book
Everything® Sex Signs Book, $9.95
Everything® Tarot Book, 2nd Ed.
Everything® Wicca and Witchcraft Book

PARENTING

Everything® Baby Names Book, 2nd Ed.
Everything® Baby Shower Book
Everything® Baby's First Food Book
Everything® Baby's First Year Book
Everything® Birthing Book
Everything® Breastfeeding Book
Everything® Father-to-Be Book
Everything® Father's First Year Book
Everything® Get Ready for Baby Book
Everything® Get Your Baby to Sleep Book, $9.95
Everything® Getting Pregnant Book
Everything® Guide to Raising a One-Year-Old
Everything® Guide to Raising a Two-Year-Old
Everything® Homeschooling Book
Everything® Mother's First Year Book
Everything® Parent's Guide to Children and Divorce
Everything® Parent's Guide to Children with ADD/ADHD
Everything® Parent's Guide to Children with Asperger's Syndrome
Everything® Parent's Guide to Children with Autism
Everything® Parent's Guide to Children with Bipolar Disorder
Everything® Parent's Guide to Children with Dyslexia
Everything® Parent's Guide to Positive Discipline
Everything® Parent's Guide to Raising a Successful Child
Everything® Parent's Guide to Raising Boys
Everything® Parent's Guide to Raising Siblings
Everything® Parent's Guide to Sensory Integration Disorder
Everything® Parent's Guide to Tantrums
Everything® Parent's Guide to the Overweight Child
Everything® Parent's Guide to the Strong-Willed Child
Everything® Parenting a Teenager Book
Everything® Potty Training Book, $9.95
Everything® Pregnancy Book, 2nd Ed.
Everything® Pregnancy Fitness Book
Everything® Pregnancy Nutrition Book
Everything® Pregnancy Organizer, 2nd Ed., $16.95
Everything® Toddler Activities Book
Everything® Toddler Book
Everything® Tween Book
Everything® Twins, Triplets, and More Book

PETS

Everything® Aquarium Book
Everything® Boxer Book
Everything® Cat Book, 2nd Ed.
Everything® Chihuahua Book
Everything® Dachshund Book
Everything® Dog Book
Everything® Dog Health Book
Everything® Dog Owner's Organizer, $16.95
Everything® Dog Training and Tricks Book
Everything® German Shepherd Book
Everything® Golden Retriever Book
Everything® Horse Book
Everything® Horse Care Book
Everything® Horseback Riding Book
Everything® Labrador Retriever Book
Everything® Poodle Book
Everything® Pug Book
Everything® Puppy Book
Everything® Rottweiler Book
Everything® Small Dogs Book
Everything® Tropical Fish Book
Everything® Yorkshire Terrier Book

REFERENCE

Everything® Blogging Book
Everything® Build Your Vocabulary Book
Everything® Car Care Book
Everything® Classical Mythology Book
Everything® Da Vinci Book
Everything® Divorce Book
Everything® Einstein Book
Everything® Etiquette Book, 2nd Ed.
Everything® Inventions and Patents Book
Everything® Mafia Book
Everything® Philosophy Book
Everything® Psychology Book
Everything® Shakespeare Book

RELIGION

Everything® Angels Book
Everything® Bible Book
Everything® Buddhism Book
Everything® Catholicism Book
Everything® Christianity Book
Everything® History of the Bible Book
Everything® Jesus Book
Everything® Jewish History & Heritage Book
Everything® Judaism Book
Everything® Kabbalah Book
Everything® Koran Book
Everything® Mary Book
Everything® Mary Magdalene Book

Everything® Prayer Book
Everything® Saints Book
Everything® Torah Book
Everything® Understanding Islam Book
Everything® World's Religions Book
Everything® Zen Book

SCHOOL & CAREERS

Everything® Alternative Careers Book
Everything® Career Tests Book
Everything® College Major Test Book
Everything® College Survival Book, 2nd Ed.
Everything® Cover Letter Book, 2nd Ed.
Everything® Filmmaking Book
Everything® Get-a-Job Book
Everything® Guide to Being a Paralegal
Everything® Guide to Being a Real Estate Agent
Everything® Guide to Being a Sales Rep
Everything® Guide to Careers in Health Care
Everything® Guide to Careers in Law Enforcement
Everything® Guide to Government Jobs
Everything® Guide to Starting and Running a Restaurant
Everything® Job Interview Book
Everything® New Nurse Book
Everything® New Teacher Book
Everything® Paying for College Book
Everything® Practice Interview Book
Everything® Resume Book, 2nd Ed.
Everything® Study Book

SELF-HELP

Everything® Dating Book, 2nd Ed.
Everything® Great Sex Book
Everything® Kama Sutra Book
Everything® Self-Esteem Book

SPORTS & FITNESS

Everything® Easy Fitness Book
Everything® Fishing Book
Everything® Golf Instruction Book
Everything® Pilates Book
Everything® Running Book
Everything® Weight Training Book
Everything® Yoga Book

TRAVEL

Everything® Family Guide to Cruise Vacations
Everything® Family Guide to Hawaii
Everything® Family Guide to Las Vegas, 2nd Ed.

Everything® Family Guide to Mexico
Everything® Family Guide to New York City, 2nd Ed.
Everything® Family Guide to RV Travel & Campgrounds
Everything® Family Guide to the Caribbean
Everything® Family Guide to the Walt Disney World Resort®, Universal Studios®, and Greater Orlando, 4th Ed.
Everything® Family Guide to Timeshares
Everything® Family Guide to Washington D.C., 2nd Ed.
Everything® Guide to New England

WEDDINGS

Everything® Bachelorette Party Book, $9.95
Everything® Bridesmaid Book, $9.95
Everything® Destination Wedding Book
Everything® Elopement Book, $9.95
Everything® Father of the Bride Book, $9.95
Everything® Groom Book, $9.95
Everything® Mother of the Bride Book, $9.95
Everything® Outdoor Wedding Book
Everything® Wedding Book, 3rd Ed.
Everything® Wedding Checklist, $9.95
Everything® Wedding Etiquette Book, $9.95
Everything® Wedding Organizer, 2nd Ed., $16.95
Everything® Wedding Shower Book, $9.95
Everything® Wedding Vows Book, $9.95
Everything® Wedding Workout Book
Everything® Weddings on a Budget Book, $9.95

WRITING

Everything® Creative Writing Book
Everything® Get Published Book, 2nd Ed.
Everything® Grammar and Style Book
Everything® Guide to Writing a Book Proposal
Everything® Guide to Writing a Novel
Everything® Guide to Writing Children's Books
Everything® Guide to Writing Research Papers
Everything® Screenwriting Book
Everything® Writing Poetry Book
Everything® Writing Well Book